Praise for
SOMETIMES THE MAGIC WORKS

"Terry Brooks is adamant about dedicating oneself to the craft, while showing awe and humility for the creative process. . . . Every serious writer should refer to this book regularly for inspiration as well as solid crafting advice."

—ELIZABETH ENGSTROM CRATTY
Director, Maui Writers Retreat

"A wise, warm-hearted book—part autobiography, part how-to-do-it manual, with some amazingly candid behind-the-scenes material . . . Fantasy fans, novice writers, and even veteran pros will learn plenty from it."

—ROBERT SILVERBERG
Award-winning author of
Majipoor Chronicles

SOMETIMES THE
MAGIC WORKS

Lessons from a Writing Life

TERRY BROOKS

DEL REY

BALLANTINE BOOKS | NEW YORK

A Del Rey ® Book
Published by The Random House Publishing Group

Copyright © 2003 by Terry Brooks
Introduction © 2003 by Elizabeth George

Published in the United States by Del Rey Books, an imprint of The Random
House Publishing Group, a division of Random House, Inc., New York, and
simultaneously in Canada by Random House of Canada Limited, Toronto.

Del Rey is a registered trademark and the Del Rey colophon is a trademark of
Random House, Inc.

www.delreybooks.com

Library of Congress Catalog Card Number: 2003098274

ISBN 978-0-345-46551-1

Text design by Richard Oriolo

Manufactured in the United States of America

First Hardcover Edition: March 2003
First Trade Paperback Edition: February 2004

CONTENTS

INTRODUCTION

by Elizabeth George

YOU ARE ABOUT to take a journey with fantasy novel-ist Terry Brooks. But unlike other journeys you may have taken with him, this one does not involve elves, fairies, and the like. Instead, Terry is going to take you into his life. More important, from my point of view, Terry is also going to take you into his work.

I believe that every long-term successful writer employs some sort of game plan when he ventures into the world of novel writing. Please note that I said *long-term* successful writer. It's true that there will always be that flash in the pan, that one-off novel that strikes the fancy of publishers, sells a few million copies, and gets made into a successful—or unsuccessful—

film before the person who wrote it fades into permanent obscurity, laughing, as they say, all the way to the bank. These types of writers have always existed. In fact, quite a few dubious works of fiction leap immediately into my mind as I write this and no doubt into yours as well. The creators of those largely forgettable and sometimes laughable pieces of prose bang them right out, often with nothing more to recommend their work than a fairly decent idea badly realized, a fairly bad idea decently realized, or a schtick of some sort—author as former policewoman, forensic pathologist, secretary posing as either, weight lifter, beauty queen, seriously abused child, seriously abusive adult come to the Lord, etc., etc., etc.—or an excellent publicity campaign that worked like a charm. What those creators of fiction have in common tends to be that they got lucky. They wrote their novels without an idea in the world about what they were doing and they managed to pull it off. Problem was, though, they could not do it again.

The difference, then, between a one-off novelist and a long-term successful writer is that the long-term writer can do it again. And again. And again. The reason for this is not a more active imagination, greater creative drive, or better luck. It is simply that the long-term successful writer has a game plan called *craft*.

Terry Brooks is just that sort of writer. With more than two decades of acclaimed commercial fiction to his credit, he does not sit down at the word processor, the typewriter, the legal pad, or the index card and hope to get in touch with the cosmos. He goes into the creative act knowing that there will be work involved—work that he is willing to do because he knows it's essential to the outcome he seeks.

If your ambition is to make millions, to sell to Hollywood,

to see Tom Cruise, Brad Pitt, and Julia Roberts on the screen enunciating your timeless dialogue, you should read no further. If you wish to join the league of one-trick ponies who are nonetheless millionaires because they were able to "get it right" just once, you should read no further. What Terry Brooks has to say in this slim volume will not satiate your appetite for instant fame and fortune because Terry Brooks is going to tell you about craft. And as any craftsman knows, that means *work*.

Terry and I have been on the same page with regard to craft since the moment we met a few years ago at the Maui Writers Conference. We both believe that novel writing is an art. We both also believe that that art must be founded on solid craft. For anyone who wants to enter into the rarefied world of the master craftsman, this is the book for you. Terry Brooks will take you on his personal journey from obscurity—no offense, Terry—to bestsellerdom, and along the route, you'll have the chance to pick up a few pointers from a man who definitely practices what he preaches.

Here's the thing about writing: There are writers and there are authors. Writers seek to write, and they seek to write better and better with every book. Authors seek only to be published, and they seek advances to match their egos. Terry Brooks is definitely the former, so you can trust what he has to say about craft. Once you've read the book, you yourself can decide which you are at the present time—writer or author— or which one you are determined to be.

Believe me, Terry will show you that there is nothing easy about writing a novel. And I will tell you here and now: There's also nothing as *satisfying* as writing a novel, either.

Enjoy.

This is for writers yet to be published who think the
uphill climb will never end. Keep believing.
This is also for published writers grown jaded by the process.
Remember how lucky you are.

The muse whispers to you when she chooses,

and you can't tell her to come back later,

because you quickly learn in this business

that she might not come back at all.

I AM NOT ALL HERE

I T'S TRUE.
I'm not all here.

One of my earliest memories is of sitting in church with Grandmother Gleason, my mother's mother, and her sister, my aunt Blanche, and listening to them discuss a woman several pews ahead of us. They did this frequently when I was with them, and they always did so in a stage whisper that could be heard by anyone within a dozen feet. The conversation went something like this:

"Blanche, isn't that Mildred Evans?"

"No! Where?"

"Sitting just ahead of us by Harold Peterson. Look at that hat she's wearing. Have you ever seen such a hat?"

"Are those birds pinned to it? They look like birds."

"I think they're finches."

"I don't think that's Mildred Walker. I think she's dead."

"Mildred *Evans*!"

"No, you're thinking of *Myrtle* Evans. Besides, I think she's dead, too. She wasn't all here, you know. Everybody said so."

By then I had sunk as far as I could into the pew, staring down at my bible and wishing I wasn't all there, either. Perhaps somewhere along the way, my wish was granted.

I don't like to examine this condition too closely, but I know that it is likely that right at this very moment one of my relatives or friends is remarking on it. When I was married, they warned my wife about it. *He's not all here*, they would say, leaning close, imparting this information with sad, knowing smiles. Judine thought they were kidding, but that was before she discovered that I only hear maybe half of what she says to me. Her favorite example of my inattention—and there are many—involves reading something to me from the newspaper about which she thinks I ought to know. I listen and nod. I might even respond. Then five minutes later, when the paper is in my hands, I will read the same item back to her as if I was just discovering it. Which I am. This happens all the time. These days, she just shakes her head helplessly.

My children think it is a big joke. They know me well enough by now not to be surprised when it happens. *Dad's gone away again*, they say to each other with a snicker. *Joe Space Cadet*. Sometimes they suggest I should get my hearing checked, that maybe the problem is I just don't hear what they have to say. I tell them I don't want to hear what they have to say because it usually involves giving them money. But these days, as the big six-oh approaches, I suppose I ought to give the poor-hearing argument a little more consideration.

Actually, my family and friends like me well enough, but they think I am weird. Or at least peculiar. I can't blame them. I should have grown up a long time ago, and yet here I am, writing about elves and magic. I should have a real job by now. I did have a real job, once upon a time. I was a lawyer for seventeen years, but I quit when I felt comfortable enough with my writing career to think I could make a living at it. Readers used to ask me at autographing events if it wasn't hard making the transition from practicing law to writing fantasy. I told them there was hardly any difference at all. That always got a laugh. They knew what I meant.

So what am I talking about when I say I am not all here? I mean that if you are a writer, you really can't be. Writers are not all here, because a part of them is always "over there"— "over there" being whatever world they are writing about at present. Writers live in two worlds—the real world of friends and family and the imaginary world of their writing. If you were to measure the difference in time spent between the two, I suspect you would find it quite small. Nor is this distinction of real and imaginary meant to suggest that for a writer one is more compelling than the other. It isn't. Each is compelling in its own way and each makes its demands on a writer's time. But a writer can't ever leave either for very long—in the case of the real world, for obvious reasons, and in the case of the imaginary world, for reasons that require a brief digression in order to make sense of them.

Let's take a momentary look at writers and their books. That writers live in their writing probably isn't news to you, but that they do so as much out of necessity as desire might be. I might argue that they do so because that is how writers are built: the writing compels and commands them as if they were little robots. They are not complete without it or happy when they aren't doing it. Writing is life; you've heard that one, haven't you? Writers need their writing; they need their imaginary worlds in order to find peace in, or make sense of, the real world.

I am always dabbling in my current book, no matter the time or place, thinking about some aspect of the writing that I haven't quite gotten right or executed well enough. It doesn't command my entire attention, just enough of it that I seem constantly distracted. Various dilemmas and concerns steal me away. Sometimes it is a character that hasn't been fully developed. Sometimes it is a plot element that just doesn't fit quite the way it should. Sometimes it is something as mundane as a name that needs rethinking. Sometimes it is your basic insecurity attack; I just know that what I have written the day before is dreck and will have to be thrown out. Sometimes I am just thinking ahead to the next day's writing and beginning to put the images together in my mind.

But it is always something, as the saying goes. There is never a moment when I am not involved in thinking about writing. I can't put it out of my mind entirely, even in the most trying of circumstances. You might as well ask me to stop breathing; thinking about my writing is as much a function of my life.

So when my family and friends discover I am not listening to them or they catch me staring off into space, I can't do a thing about it, because that's just the way I am. It is the way all writers are, I suspect. The muse whispers to you when she chooses, and you can't tell her to come back later, because you quickly learn in this business that she might not come back at all.

Some of this has to do with writers being observers. We

don't become involved so much as we watch and take notes. Much of what happens around us goes into a storage bin in our minds for future consideration and possible use in a book down the line. What we observe is as important to us in determining what we write as what we know. Frequently those annoying distractions we experience are just instances of recording our observations because we think they might suggest, on reflection, further writing possibilities.

The writer Walter Mosley wrote a few years ago in an article that appeared in the *New York Times* that writing is gathering smoke—the smoke of dreams, of ideas, of the imagination. We collect that smoke and try to make something out of it. It doesn't happen all at once, but only over time and never on a determinable schedule. We visit our hazy treasure every day in order not to lose sight of it, not to let it evaporate from neglect. At some point in our tending and examination, something substantial will come alive.

I think this is what writers are doing when that part of them that isn't here is over there. They are gathering smoke. They are thinking about their writing, trying to make something solid and recognizable out of the ether of their musings.

Some would say that a writer's most important work is to chronicle the human condition. I think that it is more important that they explore its possibilities. We don't find answers so much in what we already know as in what we think might be.

To do that, a writer has to be able to step outside the real world to the world of the imagination. By doing so, perspective is gained.

Not being all here, when viewed in that light, finally begins to make sense.

I have decided, on reflection, it is best just to

remember that sometimes the magic really works.

LUCK

IN EARLY NOVEMBER of 1974, I received a letter
from editor, writer, and critic Lester del Rey. He was re-
sponding to my submission of the manuscript for a first novel
entitled *The Sword of Shannara*. After an opening paragraph
in which he apologized for not replying more swiftly to my
query letter, he wrote the following sentence.

> *Let me say at once that I consider your novel as poten-
> tially the best epic fantasy since Tolkien's* The Lord of the
> Rings.

Heady words to bestow on a young writer aspiring to his
first publication. I didn't entirely trust them, but I was more

than willing to be seduced. I read on. He astonished me by taking time to explain who he was and what his credentials were. As if I didn't know, a reader of his books since I was twelve. He asked if I was willing to work long and hard to make my book, in its all-too-rough and still-unfinished form, a publishable piece of work. As if I wouldn't have done anything to see my words in print, on the shelves of bookstores, in the hands of readers.

I came to Lester's attention through the efforts of Donald A. Wollheim, publisher of DAW Books, to whom I had submitted the manuscript first. After reading it and ruminating on its potential, he returned it to me with the suggestion that I send it to Judy-Lynn del Rey at Ballantine Books, who had just been hired as editor in chief of the division's science fiction/fantasy line. I submitted it in time-honored fashion—over the transom, a slush-pile offering, just another roll of the dice in an endless series of rolls by would-be authors countrywide.

And now this.

A miracle.

I agreed to do what Lester asked, of course, not yet fully realizing what that would entail, but not really caring either. I received a second letter in short order, which ran for ten pages, typed and single spaced, with handwritten notes in the margins, detailing what I would need to do in the way of rewrites. It was a substantial amount of work, but I did everything he asked without complaint because by then I would have walked barefoot over hot coals if that was what it would take to ally myself with someone who believed in me.

I spent the entire next year working with Lester to improve the book. I rewrote sections repeatedly, and each time the story became a little stronger. Judy-Lynn hand-sold the book for a year after that, visiting with sales reps, booksellers, and the media to talk about its importance. She told everyone who would listen, as Lester had told me, that it might be the most important work of fantasy since *The Lord of the Rings*. I have no idea how many believed her and how many thought she was off her rocker, but at least the word got out.

Then, in an extraordinary piece of good fortune, the Literary Guild agreed to make the book a featured alternate. But the planned format for the book was not hardcover, and the Guild could not discount it unless it came out in a hardcover version. Ballantine/Del Rey was doing only a trade paperback release, so there was no help to be found within house. A determined Judy-Lynn solved the problem by persuading parent company Random House to pick up the book for a small print run in hardcover. The Literary Guild's selection was assured.

Twenty-eight months later, in April 1977, *The Sword of Shannara* was released in trade paperback and hardcover formats. My book, my dream. It did very well—better than very well. It became the first work of fiction ever to land on the *New York Times* Trade Paperback Best-Seller List, and it stayed there for over five months, most of the time in the top five. It was written up by Frank Herbert in the *New York Times Book Review*, an extraordinary event. The *New York Times* almost never bothers with fantasy and even when it does, allots no more than a paragraph. The review for *Sword* covered half a page. Neither overly enthusiastic nor unfairly critical, it was a balanced, fair assessment of a first-time author's efforts.

Thus my writing career was successfully launched.

But, as Paul Harvey would say, here is the rest of the story.

The writer Elizabeth Engstrom gives a talk in which she discusses the factors that most influence whether or not an aspiring writer will be published. At the top of her list, she places Luck. With a capital L. Let me tell you about Luck as it applies to the success of *The Sword of Shannara*.

I did not find out what I am about to relate until many years after the book was in print. By then I was no longer quite so naïve about the business, which made what I discovered all the more mind-boggling. Lester himself told me one day while we were visiting at his home in New York City. He did so in a matter-of-fact way, as if it were the most natural thing in the world. I masked my astonishment mostly because I knew I would need time to think things over later.

This is what he told me.

When I submitted my manuscript in the spring of 1974, Ron Busch, then president of Ballantine Books, had just hired Judy-Lynn del Rey to run the science fiction division. He was negotiating, through her, to hire her husband, Lester, to work for the company, as well. When Judy-Lynn received my manuscript, all eight-hundred-plus pages, she was impressed enough by the letter from Don Wollheim not to dismiss it out of hand. But her publishing background was not in fantasy; it was in science fiction. So she gave the book to Lester to read.

You have to understand Lester to appreciate what happened next. Lester was opinionated, argumentative, and a curmudgeon of the first rank. He prided himself on being able to argue any point of view and would switch sides in the middle of a debate without skipping a beat. He was also a brilliant editor. I would hear from those who worked with him over the next fifteen years that he was one of the great editors of the twentieth century. Together with Judy-Lynn, he launched successfully the careers of a dozen major fantasy and science fiction authors and resurrected or reinvented the careers of a dozen more. During the late 1970s and early 1980s, they turned Del Rey Books into the number one publisher of science fiction and fantasy.

But in 1974, before he was even hired by Ballantine as an editor, he began this crusade with *The Sword of Shannara*.

The perception in publishing at the time was that fantasy did not sell, that its readership was small and not broad based, and that the potential for expansion was limited. Yes, J. R. R. Tolkien had sold hundreds of thousands of copies of *The Lord of the Rings* and *The Hobbit*. But that was because he was J. R. R. Tolkien, and no one else was. Fantasy, as a form of category fiction, was too esoteric to be widely marketable.

Lester believed that this was horse pucky. He believed the market was huge, the readership vast and hungry, and the potential for sales enormous.

He decided to use *The Sword of Shannara* to prove his point.

He did so by telling Ron Busch that he would take the editorial position being offered. He would work with Judy-Lynn at Ballantine Books, where they would launch a science fiction/fantasy imprint. But Ron must agree to let him make *The Sword of Shannara* his first original fantasy publication and the centerpiece of the imprint's launch. Ron, who admitted to knowing little or nothing about science fiction and fantasy but who trusted the del Reys implicitly, agreed.

The end result was that Lester disproved those critics who had maintained that fantasy wouldn't sell to a large audience. *The Sword of Shannara* sold in record numbers and changed the face of publishing. I had nothing to do with any of this. I watched it all from the sidelines, as amazed as everyone else, wondering for a very long time at my incredible good fortune.

What are the odds against things working out in so serendipitous a fashion? Enormous, of course. It is the prototypical case of being in the right place at the right time. Six months earlier or later with my submission, and I would have been out of luck.

Luck, with a capital L.

Ultimately, I am conflicted. I was used as a guinea pig so that Lester could prove a point. The book was published precisely because it was so similar to Tolkien's work, and for many critics and readers that was an unforgivable transgression. As a result, I was savaged in many quarters. Lester was not the least bit troubled by this. The reviews and commentaries were sent to me, good and bad. He dismissed them all, telling me to keep them, to give them the momentary attention they deserved and no more, and to remember that no matter what anyone said, *Sword* was a "damn good book."

At the time, I took it in stride. After all, the book sold well, so what did it matter if a few critics didn't like it? Well, more than a few. The experience helped form my view of what it means to be a commercial fiction writer. It thickened my skin. Only later, when I learned the truth about how the book got picked up and anointed for special treatment, did I take time to wonder at the capriciousness of being published.

A month before the release of *The Sword of Shannara*, I attended a launch party in New York City for the Del Rey imprint and met both Lester del Rey and Don Wollheim for the first time. I heard Lester tell Don that he owed the latter a dinner for sending over the manuscript for *The Sword of Shannara*. I heard Don reply that Lester owed him a good deal more than that.

How much, then, do I owe Lester? And Judy-Lynn? Even

after all this time, I have no idea how to calculate it. Conflicted or not by what I later learned, it is considerable. If my book was a driven man's experiment, it was a successful one. I do not feel cheated or betrayed. The book was a labor of love for all of us, whatever our respective motives. Lester proved his point, Judy-Lynn had her launch, and I had my dream fulfilled.

Not too shabby.

I have decided, on reflection, it is best just to remember that sometimes the magic really works.

I am incomplete without my work. I am so closely bound to it, so much identified by it, that without it I think I would crumble into dust and drift away.

WHY I WRITE

JUDINE BELIEVES THAT fiction writers are born to their calling. She believes that genetic makeup determines if you are suited to write stories for a living. Even if you decide that this is what you want to do with your life, you won't be successful if your genes don't allow for it.

I understand her point. Maybe you have to live with a writer to understand why she feels as she does. Fiction writers are strange beasts. They are, like all writers, observers first and foremost. Everything that happens to and around them is potential material for a story, and they look at it that way. I am no different. I see something happen, read or hear about an event, and the first question that pops into my mind is, How can I use that in a story?

The strangeness doesn't stop there. Who else do you know who lives life in two worlds on a regular basis? Fiction writers do. I have already said so. They live in the real world and whatever world they are writing about at the same time. They go back and forth between the two at the drop of a hat. What happens in the first suggests what might happen in the second. Daydreaming takes on an entirely new meaning. I am particularly bad about this. I can go away from a conversation in an instant, leaving this world for the one in which I am working, lost in an idea or a plot development. It happens at parties. It happens in the middle of conversations. I don't have any control over it, and I am not sure I want to. I think it is the source of my creativity, and I don't want to disrupt the process.

It may be that writers are actually happier living in their books than they are in the real world. There is evidence of this in the way writers immerse themselves in their fiction. How many times have you heard it said about someone that they are happiest at their work? Writers are like that, whether they admit it or not. But while most jobs fall into the nine-to-five category, fiction writing is a twenty-four-hour-a-day occupation. You never leave your work behind. It is always with you, and to some extent, you are always thinking about it. You don't take your work home; your work never leaves home. It lives inside you. It resides and grows and comes alive in your mind.

Whatever the behavioral propensities of writers and regardless of the prerequisite of a proper genetic makeup, they still have to find their way to their craft. I suspect that there are as many ways of this happening as there are stories of being published. Since I cannot speak for other writers in this matter, except to the extent that their experiences are the same as mine, I shall stick to what brought me into the fold.

I submit that it has mostly to do with how I grew up. But you must judge for yourselves.

I was born in a small midwestern town in the mid-1940s. Sterling, Illinois, had a population of about fifteen thousand and was situated directly across the Rock River from the city of Rock Falls with a population of about ten thousand. They were essentially steel towns settled in the middle of farm country about a hundred miles west of Chicago. My father, back from the war, worked at a small printing company where he was the junior partner. My mother was a housewife. They weren't Ozzie and Harriet, but they weren't all that different either.

Because my growing up took place during the late 1940s and early 1950s, my life was different from that of today's kids. I know. Duh. But I mean *really* different. Allow me to illustrate. There weren't any computers or video games. There weren't any videos. There weren't tape players or CDs. Television was a luxury. There wasn't a television in my house until I was six, and even then it didn't offer much programming for kids; Saturday mornings and after-school serials were about it. There were movie matinees every Saturday afternoon, but nothing midweek or at night. Mostly, there was radio, comics, and books.

I can see it in your eyes. *How old is he?*

There wasn't a lot in the way of kids' toys either, so even if you had the money, which most of us didn't, there wasn't much to choose from in any case. There was very little toy merchandising connected with television or movies. No one had tapped into that gold mine yet, and the world probably wasn't ready for it anyway.

Mostly, kids were expected to entertain themselves and

stay out of their parents' hair. To that end, you were sent out-side to play at the drop of a hat. It wasn't an option; it was a standing mandate. If there wasn't a winter blizzard or a spring rainstorm or a summer heat wave, you went outside and stayed outside until the next mealtime came around.

The neighborhood I grew up in was my designated play-ground. My boundaries were carefully laid out—west to Ave-nue J, east to Avenue G, south to 12th Street, and north to the cornfield, which at that time was somewhere around 16th Street. All of my friends lived within the perimeter of these bound-aries, and we all hung out together. Today's concerns about let-ting kids wander around alone didn't exist. Everyone in the neighborhood knew who you were and kept an eye on you when you were within shouting distance, and you were always within shouting distance of someone because in those days women mostly were housewives and stayed home.

What did we do for fun? Well, we tried to stay out of trou-ble, of course, although I'm not sure that any of us ever fig-ured out exactly how to do that. We invented our fun from what we knew, and what we knew came mostly from the aforemen-tioned books, radio programs, and comics. We all read the same comics and listened to the same radio serials. We saw pretty much the same movies. We read different books, but mostly on the same subjects. We were impressed by these sto-ries and played at being the characters. We would establish a story and improve on it. We were knights in armor one day and soldiers the next, cowboys and Indians one week, Sergeant Preston and his Mounties the next. We were anything and everything, and we invented role-playing before there was even a name for it.

The results were mixed. Some games were better than others. We had a great World War II version of Capture the Flag going for several weeks one summer. The Three Mesquiteers—Bob Livingston, Ray Corrigan, and Max Terhune—dominated a couple more. But when we cut off broom handles for lances, took up metal garbage can lids for shields, and ran at each other on our bikes like the knights of King Arthur, we knew we were on to something. Unfortunately, my mother glanced out the kitchen window, saw what we were doing, and quickly intervened. We talked about the possibility of hanging Frankie Clements after seeing *The Ox-Bow Incident.* It was his brother's idea, I should hasten to point out. Frankie didn't seem to mind; heck, he was eager to try it. I mean, we weren't really going to hang him; we were only going to pretend. But his mother wasn't very understanding when she found out what we were planning. She sent her own kids up to their rooms and the rest of us packing for home. I don't know about the other kids, but the inevitable follow-up phone call to my parents got me just the sort of lecture you would expect.

When I was only five or six, I spent three days tracking a bobcat through the neighborhood. I can't remember now how I learned about the bobcat, only that I did and I was sure it was coming our way. After all, it was sighted only two counties over. It was winter, and I found its paw prints in the fresh snow right away. Biggest cat tracks you ever saw. There was no doubt about what it was. I never actually caught up to it, but for those three days that I tried, I lived right on the edge of a heart attack every time I rounded a corner.

When I was not playing outside, I played up in my room. The rules changed, but the games were the same. Because we didn't have our outdoor space, we had to give up our live-action adventures and go to figures. I had hundreds of them.

Some were from sets, some came with plastic models, and some were paper cutouts backed on cardboard. All doubled at being more than one type of character and none ended up being used as the manufacturer envisioned. Weeks of *20,000 Leagues Under the Sea* utilized mostly World War II figures and some clay models. A Roy Rogers western set was used for everything from Zane Grey to *Black Stallion.*

It didn't really matter. We weren't in Camelot or Tombstone or aboard the *Nautilus* or anywhere but up in our rooms or outside in the neighborhood. What we created was inside our heads, because that was where it was most real. That was where it came alive.

But mostly it came alive for me. My friends played at these games, but they didn't live them the way I did. I thought about them all the time. I was involved enough that I was content to play them alone, assuming all the roles. I was constantly reworking the story and redeveloping the characters. This fixation with playacting went on for a long time, and I know in the end, as high school neared, that my parents were beginning to despair. They didn't say so, but I could tell what they were thinking. They were thinking I was not entirely normal.

What saved me was writing. Eventually, adventures with role-playing and figures became too confining and too predictable. I wanted a larger playground, and the only one that seemed sufficiently large was inside my head. I gained an inkling of the possibilities in the fourth grade when I wrote my first story. It was about a group of boys who accepted a dare to stay overnight in a haunted house and encountered aliens. The story earned an A grade. I was hooked. There were others after that, and somewhere along the way I decided that this was what I really wanted to do. I loved writing stories. I loved the puzzle-solving aspect of the process. I loved creating my own worlds, big and bright and colorful, the possibilities captivating and endless.

I didn't begin by writing about elves. First I had to write a few dog and horse stories, then a few science fiction stories, a western or two, a war story, and finally a story about a great white whale. I didn't finish any of them and none of them were very good. Nothing I wrote came out exactly the way I wanted it to. I can admit that now, safely removed from the immediacy of the pain such an admission would have cost me then. I had a story to tell, a really good story—I knew I did— but I could not seem to discover what it was.

The problem, I eventually discovered, was that I didn't want to write stories set in the real world. The real world wasn't large enough or strange enough for me to work in. I needed a place that was so enormous and so different that no one but me could even begin to define it. It could not exist anywhere outside my mind except in the words I wrote. It needed to be about places we knew, but about places we didn't, as well. It needed to be about us, but about other people, too. Everything I wrote about had to remind readers of what they already knew, yet make them take a second look at whether or not what they believed was really true.

Writing is habit-forming. It is addictive. You get caught up in the challenge of the storytelling process. You become en-chanted with the worlds and characters you create. The worlds are your home and the characters your friends. You come to know both as well as you know yourself. Born of you, they be-come a part of you.

What is interesting to me now, more than forty years after

that first story, is how deeply enmeshed I am in what I do. It is beyond reasonable. If I don't write, I become restless and ill-tempered. I become dissatisfied. My reaction to not writing is both physical and emotional. I am incomplete without my work. I am so closely bound to it, so much identified by it, that without it I think I would crumble into dust and drift away.

One of my writer friends has an ironclad rule about her work. She writes five pages every day—no matter where she is or what she is doing. It doesn't matter if she is sick. It doesn't matter if she has to get up and write at four in the morning. She does it. I understand why. She is afraid that if she doesn't, she will lose her identity and her presence and disintegrate. She is the sum of her words. She is her writing.

I expect that is why Judine feels so strongly about writers and genetics. If you have a better explanation, feel free to let her know.

The point of book signings is not to make you feel
good about yourself. It is not to rack up huge sales
of your work while you stand by beaming benevolently
on an audience of clearly enlightened readers.

It's Not about You

THE SWORD OF *Shannara* was on the market for maybe six minutes when I started asking Lester del Rey about doing autographings. Oh sure, I was going to sign at the local Waldenbooks, but how about something more exciting? But Lester did not believe in book tours or public appearances for first-time authors, no matter how successful the book. Authors who had written only a single book should stay home and concentrate on writing a second, he advised me more than once. I did not argue the point. I lacked a frame of reference from which to do so. I relied on him to tell me what was best. When he told me I should stay home and write, I believed that was what I should do.

So I was somewhat surprised when I was dispatched in midsummer of the same year to Northwestern University in Chicago, a two-hour drive from my home in Sterling, to do an afternoon signing with science fiction author A. J. Budrys. I approached the event with a mix of trepidation and excitement. I was hungry for the experience, but fearful of coming off badly in front of an established and well-regarded fellow writer. After all, A. J. had done autographings hundreds of times and I was still trying to figure out exactly how they were supposed to work. I didn't want to appear like a complete idiot to someone I admired.

A. J. was there to greet me when I arrived, jovial and welcoming, aware of my uncertainty and anxious to do what he could to banish it. The book signing was being held in the university bookstore, and we sat side by side at a table near the back, facing out across a rather broad open space toward windows that opened onto the campus. We could see students walking around outside. They could see us sitting at the table inside. I reassured myself that I was prepared to meet and greet those who would stop in to buy my book.

Copies of *The Sword of Shannara* were piled in front of me, mostly in the trade paperback format, which constituted the larger printing. There were a few hardcovers, but not many. This was perfectly normal, A. J. advised, surmising my concern. This was a university, after all; no one had money for hardcovers other than textbooks. I nodded agreeably. A. J. was the professional. He had published both long and short fiction, and he knew the ropes. I couldn't help noticing that his books made an impressive display on his side of the table. I felt a bit inadequate with my solitary offering, but reminded myself that I was new to this game while he had been a published writer for many years.

A long time passed and no one came. No one even came close. A. J. commented that summer wasn't the best time to conduct an autographing on a college campus since the student population was way down. The publicity for this event was a bit Spartan, as well, he added. A notice pinned to a bulletin board here and there—that was pretty much the extent of it. Apparently the signing was thrown together in something of a hurry. I decided not to ask why.

More time passed, and still no one came. A. J. and I talked about science fiction and writing, which helped to ease my discomfort. Nevertheless, when at last someone did approach, they went straight to him and bought three of his paperbacks without a glance in my direction. I was envious in spite of myself. Then, another student appeared. This one said hello, but didn't give my book a second glance. He bought one of A. J.'s hardcovers. When he left, I raised a suspicious eyebrow at A. J. A. J. just shrugged.

Finally, after what seemed an interminable amount of time, a young woman came over and stood in front of me, looking down at my book. The conversation that followed went something like this:

SHE: Did you write this book?

ME: Uh.

A.J.: This is Terry Brooks. This is his first publication, an epic fantasy. It's a terrific story. If you haven't heard about it yet, you will soon. It was on all the best-seller lists earlier this year. I read it and enjoyed it, and I think you will, too. Take a look at the cover.

SHE: Is it science fiction?

ME: Uh.

A.J.: No, it's fantasy. You've read J. R. R. Tolkien, haven't you? It's like that, with elves and dwarves and magic, a quest and a coming of age, really terrific.

A. J. went on from there at great length, trying to sell her the book on my behalf. He extolled its virtues and lauded my inaugural writing effort. He told her all about the different formats, the artwork by the Brothers Hildebrandt, and the importance of getting in on the ground floor of what he was certain would be a classic. He did everything but offer her coupons. I was enormously grateful. Even after all of this, I was still having trouble getting two words out in support of myself.

Finally A. J. finished, having said everything he could to close the sale. I took a deep breath and crossed my fingers. I wanted this much worse than I had thought I would.

The young woman put the book back down and smiled at me.

"Have you written anything else?" she asked.

She left without buying the book. No one else even looked at it for the rest of the time I was there. A. J. and I exchanged addresses and phone numbers at the close, and I drove home in a decided funk, my imagination kicking into overdrive. My fifteen minutes of fame were up. My career was at an end. My writing life was over.

I thought like this because I had missed completely the point of the lesson I had just been taught.

There would be other signings like this one—more than a few—where only a handful of people showed up and few, if any, books were sold. This would happen even after I had a dozen best-sellers in print. It would happen with *Star Wars: The Phantom Menace*. After three signings in Salt Lake City where the crowds were so large I spent almost five exhausting hours at each venue, I flew to California the next day for a midday signing at a Wal-Mart where not a dozen people showed.

There is no help for it. It is an inescapable part of a writer's public life. Sometimes, no matter who you are or how well planned the event, people stay home or go elsewhere. You learn to accept that every time you agree to make an appearance, things might not work out the way you would like. You do not take it personally, because there is no point in doing so. No one involved wants a book signing to be a failure. Not even those people who choose to stay home or go elsewhere want to see you disheartened or angry. They are simply making a choice about how to spend their time and money. Sometimes you get the benefit of their largesse; sometimes you don't. You have to respect that the choice is theirs to make.

Here is what is important about book signings. It is a lesson I have learned over the years, one that helps me deal with virtually any adverse situation I encounter. The point of book signings is not to make you feel good about yourself. It is not to rack up huge sales of your work while you stand by beaming benevolently on an audience of clearly enlightened readers. It is not even about advancing your career—at least, not in a direct sort of way.

It is not, in fact, about you at all.

Rather, it is about making a connection between readers and books. It is about making readers feel so enthusiastic about books that they cannot wait to come back and buy more—not just copies of your books, but of other authors' books, as well. It is about generating a feeling of goodwill toward the bookstore and the staff. Mostly, it is about reassuring everyone that they did not waste their time on you.

How do you accomplish this? It is unexpectedly easy, once

you understand the dynamics of an autographing. Believe it or not, success or failure is entirely up to you. Your attitude will set the tone for everything that happens. You are the one in control. If you don't understand this, stay home until you figure it out. It is your obligation to be cheerful and welcoming toward everyone you encounter, from the staff of the bookstore to the readers who buy your book to the customers who don't. If you are, there is a better than even chance that they will be cheerful back. Didn't we learn this on *Mister Rogers' Neighborhood* about a gazillion years ago? Speak to everyone. Make them aware of the fact that you are grateful to be there, anxious to chat, and ready to answer questions if they have any. Never sign a book without looking at and speaking directly to the reader, and then thank them for choosing to take a chance on you.

Think about it. How can you not do this? Every one of those people has come out to meet you because they love your work. Or if they are there purely by chance, your response to them might determine whether or not you end up with a new reader. Either way, they are paying you a compliment. They are giving up their time and maybe their money for you. You are the only one who can make them feel it was worthwhile for them to do so.

The staff of the bookstore will appreciate this, too. They want to know something about you, a writer whose work they sell. You owe them that opportunity. You owe them your thanks. You owe them a good experience for their customers, who will come back to this store remembering what meeting you was like. If the experience is a good one, everything that surrounds it tends to be remembered as having been good, too. The staff of the bookstore will remember how you conducted yourself, no matter whether two people appeared or two hundred. They will remember you when someone asks for your books. Perhaps they will suggest your book when a customer asks for a recommendation for a new author.

This is not always easy. Disappointments and discouragement await us as authors at every turn. We set ourselves up in anticipation of being knocked down. Someone is always ready and willing to tell us how our books could have been done better. Someone is always close at hand to point out how we failed. Our self-esteem is closely tied to our writing, and someone is always ready to step on it. That, too, is part of the territory. But understanding what it is that we are trying to accomplish when we throw off our solitary trappings long enough to face our public at a book signing will make us better able to set a balance to whatever happens.

Looking at it like this, it becomes clear that the failure of some twenty-five years ago lies not with the young woman who chose to pass up the chance to buy my book, but with me. I am the one who reacted badly. I am the one who based success or failure entirely on whether or not a sale was made instead of a connection formed. It is a hard lesson, but an important one. I have never forgotten it.

I like to think that the young woman eventually thought better of her decision not to buy a copy of my book. I like to think she went back and bought it later, became an avid reader of the entire series, and ultimately introduced it to her children. I like to think she became a huge fan.

Which explains, I suppose, why I find it so easy to write fantasy.

I cannot imagine life without books any more than
I can imagine life without breathing.

INFLUENCES

I HAVE ALWAYS wanted to be a writer.

There might have been a time very early on when I wanted to be a cowboy or a fireman, but I can't remember it. I know I liked playing at being cowboys and firemen, but I don't think I ever felt that I wanted to be either so badly that I couldn't live if I didn't find a way to do so.

But that was exactly how I felt about being a writer. Once I knew enough about life to understand that I had to grow up and actually do something besides play with toys, writing was what I wanted to do. I don't know if that realization happened all at once, but I suspect it pretty much did. What matters is that it might not have happened at all if it weren't for a handful of people who, for a variety of reasons, encouraged me in my efforts.

My parents were always my biggest boosters, enormously supportive of my efforts, often without reason for being so beyond the generally held belief that this was what parents were supposed to do. They praised my early efforts as special and indicative of real promise, when I suspect they were quite ordinary. They indulged my passion for playing with figures and making cutouts for storyboards long after they thought that I should be out playing baseball or riding my bike. They put up with my imaginings and playacting and general strangeness as if it were all perfectly normal. When I was desperate for advice on what I needed to do to improve my writing, they managed to find a children's book editor out of Detroit who gave me just enough encouragement to keep me going.

Mostly, they set an example. They read books in a way that suggested right from the beginning that I should want to do so, as well—not because reading books was a requirement, but because it was a privilege. Books were the source of such happiness and contentment that there could be no better experience. I can remember watching them read, so absorbed in their books that I could sit there making faces at them and they would not notice. There were books everywhere in our home, and while some were placed high up on the shelves, out of reach of children, I was never told I couldn't read one once I had it in my hands, even when I knew they probably weren't always thrilled by my choice.

My father was a story doctor for a time in the thirties, before the war, for a periodical called *Story* magazine. His job was to read and correct pieces of fiction that had been accepted for publication. He was essentially a line editor, but frequently was called upon to rewrite prose that needed help in order to make the story publishable. Often, the problem was severe enough that it was necessary for him to rewrite the story completely.

I found out some years later that he had wanted to be a fiction writer himself. He was nearly eighty years of age when he told me this, and just beginning to reveal some of the secrets he had kept hidden from me for many years. He had tried his hand at writing fiction, but nothing had ever come of it. I asked him not long before he died why he hadn't kept at it, and he told me, rather ruefully, that he didn't think that his writing was good enough to have bothered.

By then, there was some tension between us, and I think it was caused at least in part by my success. He was seeing in me something of what he could have been. He was happy for me, but a bit sad for himself, as well. Unfulfilled dreams are not easily forgotten. It made me wonder how much encouragement he had received in his writing efforts. Had there been someone there for him as he had been there for me? He had lived through the trials of the Depression and World War II. Demands had been made of him that had not been made of me. Had things been different, he might have pursued his writing more aggressively. I have read some of his work, now that he is gone. It is pretty good.

My mother was a writer, as well, but only sporadically and always in secret. She kept a journal, and after she died my father gave it to me to read. It was the first time I knew she had written anything. It was a typical series of entries chronicling events that had been important to my mother—visits to relatives and friends, trips abroad, and observations about her life. It showed she had a way with language and an eye for detail, but it was oddly unrevealing about her as a person. I wondered why that was. She was outgoing and loved conversation. Her writing did not suggest this.

Mostly, these writings of my parents made me wonder about my genetics, about whether my enthusiasm was in some way inherited. It seems almost impossible to believe it wasn't.

After my parents, teachers influenced me most. That piece of fiction about aliens inhabiting a haunted house was written in the fourth grade for Mrs. Dawn. She was a spark plug of energy and encouragement to her students, a woman who always seemed happy and anxious to get on with whatever she was doing. What I remember most about her class was how much fun it was. Everything we did was exciting and different, from the model of the pueblo village we built of mud on a sheet of plywood to the stories we wrote and read in class. She never told us what to write and never told us afterwards that we shouldn't have written it. She seemed to understand that at ten years of age it was important just to learn to love writing.

In the seventh grade, I had Mrs. Wylie for English. She was small, perky, sharp-eyed, and full of enthusiasm. She let us write and put on plays. We divided into groups, conceived our spectacles, dressed in costumes, and acted them out. Everyone participated. It made the books we read come alive in a new way.

Mrs. Hill, my English teacher in my freshman year of high school, rescued my first real effort at writing a book, a space opera about a trip to the moon, from my Latin teacher. The latter took it away, quite properly, because I was working on it during her class, and refused to return it afterwards. She said, in fact, that she intended to burn it. Mrs. Hill, reading the panic in my voice as I begged her to intervene, did so without hesitation and thus kept my efforts alive long enough for me to finish writing it, the first long piece of fiction I ever wrote and an important milestone.

Finally, there was Miss Dickson. She was my Advanced English teacher for my junior and senior years of high school. Everyone was afraid of her, including me. She was tough and demanding, and it was no secret that she thought girls better students than boys. Both years, in classes of more than thirty, I was one of only four boys. I feared the worst each time and was not disappointed. I struggled for my grades. But I also learned more than I had ever learned before about books and writing. I was challenged in ways that made me so much better as a writer it is difficult to describe them all. She taught me to think a story through. She insisted on outlining, which taught me to organize. She chose difficult books and made us discuss what they meant, even when we thought they didn't mean much of anything. She refused to let us sit silent. She made us write a paper every single week.

A professor of English in college would introduce me to William Faulkner. A girl I was dating would give me a copy of Tolkien's *The Lord of the Rings*. A speech on the importance of writing by author and poet James Dickey would kindle a fire inside me that would keep me hungry and eager to write for years afterwards. He would also teach me what it felt like to have to pay for an author's signature after I had bought the book.

But it was the teachers of my elementary and high school years who made the real difference in my commitment to and love of writing. They were the ones who made everything I wanted so badly seem possible. They were the ones who made me believe.

I am often asked who influences me now, so many years later, twenty-odd books down the road. All those people from my past are gone, or nearly so. My relationships in the publishing business are mostly professional and keep me at arm's length. I am expected to do well, to write regularly, to sell and keep selling. But without the fire of those early years to sustain me, how could I continue to do that? It isn't enough just to be paid to write. You have to love it, as well.

The short answer to the question of influences in the present is that I am inspired, still and always, by other books and writers. My intense love affair with books continues unabated, undiminished, and thankfully unsated to this day. I don't think that will ever change. I think books define me. I am constantly on the prowl for something new and wonderful to read. I don't care who wrote it or where it came from. I don't care what it is about. I don't care if it is fiction or nonfiction or something in between. I just want it to be wonderful. It must be a story that moves me. It must be a story that reveals incontrovertible truths about the people who are in it. Above all, it must be a story that makes me want to go directly back to my computer and write something just as good.

Oddly enough, I am not particularly influenced by writers in my own field. No one ever seems to write the kind of story I want to write, or if they come close, it isn't written in the way I would have written it. I am inspired by the best of them to write something equally wonderful, but never to write anything similar. I don't know why that is. Friends who are fantasy authors sometimes studiously avoid reading their peers so as not to be influenced. I don't worry about it. I find that almost all of my ideas and concepts and themes do not come from stories that have anything to do with what I write. To give you a concrete example, a book I have read on the difficulties of protection of the environment might suggest something about how the loss of magic in the *Shannara* world could trigger deterioration of its life-forms. That's a big stretch, but one I am quite comfortable making. The connections are never direct for me. They always require translation or mutation of some sort in order to take shape.

I am a sucker for a writer who does wonderful things with words and language, who creates images that are indelible and evocative. I will read any story where the author conjures up magic through fresh demands on my sometimes jaded imagination. Make me see something through fresh eyes, and I will follow you anywhere. Give me a reason to work a little at the pictures you are drawing with your words, and I will believe in what you tell me.

Books influence me; writers influence me. My parents and my teachers are gone. Lester is gone. Many of the people who were crucial to my success as a writer are gone. But books and writers live on, an endless stream of stories and storytellers waiting for me to jump into the current of their words, to swim through their images, and to be swept away in their flow. I cannot imagine life without books any more than I can imagine life without breathing.

I don't expect that this will ever change.

Looking back, I know that I learned more about the craft of writing and about being a writer through that one experience than I learned from all the other writing experiences of my life combined.

TOUGH LOVE

A YEAR AFTER the publication of *The Sword of Shannara*, I was hard at work on a second book and in deep trouble. Lester had been asking to see the book, or some part, or even an outline for months, but I had told him I would rather not submit anything until it was done. The trouble was that I could not seem to finish it. The ending, in particular, kept eluding me, no matter how diligently I tried to conjure it up. I had written more than 375 pages, and still something about it was not quite right.

The book was a sequel to *Sword*. I did not write *Sword* with the expectation of doing a sequel, but as soon as I finished my editing and it was ready for publication, Judy-Lynn suggested, rather too casually, that I should already be at work on the next book in the series. I did not come over on a load of coal, as my father liked to say, so I began work at once. The second book featured Rone Leah, a descendent of one of the main characters in the first, as protagonist. The title of the book was *The Song of Lorelei*. Lorelei was a young woman who could work enchantment with her singing. Her powers were immense, but her past was dark and filled with deadly secrets. In chapter five or so, she was stolen away by a mysterious intruder while under the protection of Rone Leah. The rest of the book focused on Rone's attempts to find and rescue her. Nothing was what it seemed, of course.

All well and good, I thought. But almost four hundred pages into the book, with the secrets mostly revealed and the need for a resolution of the plot and the fates of the characters clearly at hand, I was lost. I decided that giving Lester a crack at breaking the logjam was the easiest and most efficient way to resolve the matter. He was a genius at picking out weak areas and devising ways of shoring up failing plotlines. Some rewriting would be necessary, of course, but it was better to get it out of the way now. Besides, I was anxious to hear how he felt about the parts that I considered strong.

So I sent it off to him, asking for suggestions on how to finish the book and get it ready for publication.

I waited a long time for a response. I knew he would write rather than call; he had advised me early on in our relationship that he preferred to communicate with his writers in this fashion. Letters allowed time and space for a writer's contemplation of an editor's comments and criticisms. They facilitated a more balanced consideration of the changes an editor felt necessary. I understood this, even though I did not believe that talking all this over by telephone would upset me.

I was about to discover how badly I had misjudged myself. When the long-awaited letter arrived, it was nothing of what I had anticipated. Lester told me that *The Song of Lorelei* was a mess. He had considered it from as many angles as he could, and after doing so must advise me that there was no way it could be salvaged. Although it would be hard, I must let go of this effort and start over. I could ignore him if I chose. Certainly the success of *The Sword of Shannara* had opened enough publishing doors that someone would accept the book as I had written it and it might even do well based on the expectations of readers of *Sword*. But it was a bad book, and if I went this route, I would live to regret it.

I was devastated. I could not believe he had rejected it out of hand, that he had found nothing about it worth salvaging. I was in such pain that I could hardly bear it, my disappointment crushing. For several days I sulked, working my way through a gamut of emotions, mulling over a series of inappropriate responses. I kept the news to myself, but I was so low that no matter where I went or whose company I kept, I was constantly looking up at the proverbial snake's belly.

Then Judy-Lynn called to ask how I was. *Are you all right, Brooks?* She always called me by my last name, and it felt like a term of endearment when she said it. I knew what she expected me to say, and I said it. I was fine. I was handling it. Of course, I was lying through my teeth. Perhaps she sensed that. She told me that these things happen, particularly with second books, and I shouldn't despair. Nor should I take Lester's comments personally. (How else should I take them? I wanted to ask, but didn't.) Lester is doing what he must to make me a better writer, and I should listen to what he says. In fact, he is sending along some comments about the manuscript for me to consider. I shouldn't do anything more about *Lorelei* until I received those comments and had a chance to look them over.

She was encouraging and kind, and I knew she meant well. But after she hung up, I wanted to scream. I was looking for a lifeline for my sinking ship of a manuscript, and I had been tossed a bag of leaden platitudes. Nothing she had said made me feel one bit better or offered even the faintest hope that somehow, someway, I could resurrect what I now perceived to be my fading career.

I remained miserable to myself and to everyone around me for at least another week, all the while contemplating ways to get around Lester's rejection letter. I told myself that it was only one man's opinion. He didn't know everything, after all. He was a curmudgeon and so opinionated that at times I wanted to tape what he said and play it back to him later, just to let him hear himself. He might be wrong this time. Isn't everyone wrong, now and then? Maybe it was his turn. The book had problems, I knew, but simply to throw the whole thing out . . .

And on and on.

What arrived finally was nothing short of astonishing, although I did not recognize it for what it was right away. Lester had returned my manuscript almost exactly as I had submitted it. There were a few comments in the margins, a little marking up of the text, but not much of anything else written on the pages. Instead, there were pieces of yellow tablet paper inserted throughout, one about every three or four pages, filled with Lester's handwriting. In his cover letter, he asked me to read through the manuscript one more time carefully, considering his evaluation of the problems it contained as I went. He asked that I make no judgments until I had finished.

I felt irritated and threatened at first. I did not want to hear all the things he thought were wrong with my masterpiece. It was like enduring the death of a thousand cuts. But there was no help for it. If I was to find a way out of this mess, if I was to find a way to make him change his mind, I had to read in detail what he thought was wrong, so that then I could dispute him.

So I did as he asked. I began to read the text, stopping where there were inserts to read his evaluations. I had made up my mind about what I would find and how I would deal with it—but a funny thing happened. I found that I changed my mind almost at once. Lester's comments were concise, thoughtful, and right on target. I could see my mistakes. I grew less angry and more intrigued as I progressed. My mistakes multiplied like rabbits. They were everywhere, and they were obvious. I was astonished at how much I had assumed was working in my story and how little actually was. I was looking for arguments to offer in defense of my choices, for leverage to persuade Lester to change his mind, and I could not find a one.

In the end, my thinking was transformed. Lester was right; I must abandon this story. After careful consideration, I could find no way to salvage it. Worse, I was so close to the material that any attempt to scavenge from it would be disastrous. Putting aside my disappointment and frustration, I released my death grip on the material and started over.

This decision led me to write *The Elfstones of Shannara*, a book that readers repeatedly tell me they consider my best. (It presents a whole new dilemma when you are told you did your best work twenty years ago, but we will leave consideration of that for another time.) It required two years of work to complete an initial manuscript of more than six hundred pages, and when I submitted it to Lester he told me to rewrite the middle two hundred. I did so without a word of protest. I never once during this time even glanced at *The Song of Lorelei*. Later, I used Rone Leah and some of the other characters and a few of the settings while writing the third book in the series, *The Wishsong of Shannara*. But I took nothing from the plot or the underlying thematic structure of the earlier story. I had learned my lesson.

That was a long time ago. What I remember most strongly now about that experience was how amazed I was after rereading the manuscript and considering Lester's accompanying comments. I can't begin to imagine how much time and effort he must have put into going through all 375-plus pages of *Lorelei*, writing out his thoughts as he did so on those scraps of yellow tablet paper each step of the way. What he had given me was the kind of education young writers can only dream about—the kind you hope and pray you might find in college writing programs, writing conferences, or even from editors, but seldom do.

Looking back, I know that I learned more about the craft of writing and about being a writer through that one experience than I learned from all the other writing experiences of my life combined. It did not begin or end there. I was required to complete substantial rewrites on both *Sword* and *Wishsong*, the books that preceded and followed *Elfstones*. I rewrote a good chunk of *Magic Kingdom for Sale*, as well, which followed. But the heart and soul of what I know and who I am as a writer was formed in the crucible of that single experience.

There are writers who will tell you how difficult Lester del Rey was to work with. Some remember him as harsh and sometimes arbitrary. Some remember him as impossible to reason with. Some grew weary of their constant struggle to protect the integrity of their material and departed for other houses. Some still just shake their heads when his name is mentioned and utter a few choice words under their breath.

I will never be one of them.

Lester carried a card that he handed out to everyone. I still have one. It reads: *Lester del Rey, Expert.*

You might get an argument on the validity of that claim from others, but you won't get one from me.

Trying to explain in rational, analytical fashion how
we come up with our plots and our thematic structures
threatens in an odd sort of way to reveal that we are
all just humbugs hiding behind a velvet curtain.

WHERE DO YOU
GET YOUR IDEAS?

I T I S T H E most frequently asked question of writers, particularly writers of speculative fiction. It is asked at virtually every book signing, appearance, and interview. It is a legitimate question, one in which readers have a bona fide interest. They are curious to know how writers come up with all those wondrous, unusual, and intriguing concepts that comprise the framework for their stories.

But writers don't like this question. They don't like it because they hear it all the time and after a while it becomes such a cliché that they want to run screaming into the night. They don't like it because it is hard to answer. Ideas don't just happen. They don't come out of a catalogue or the phone book. They don't arrive propitiously in our dreams. (Well, now and then maybe, but I would hate to have to rely on dreams to make my deadlines.)

Writers don't like this question most of all because they are a little afraid of it. Writers are not necessarily superstitious, but they do tend to be a bit wary. Particularly about themselves and their craft. They don't quite trust it. They are leery of looking at it too closely. Examining how it works might leech away a little of its magic. Analyzing it might make the entire process too claustrophobic to bear. Most writers tend to rely heavily on intuition and gut instinct, a sort of freewheeling approach to creativity. The writer's mind might lock up with the realization that he does things in certain ways and for certain reasons, and his intuition and gut instinct might turn to stone. For the same reason, writers do not like to talk about what they are writing or intend to write until it is actually written. I am bad enough about this that I have forbidden my editor to discuss any aspect of a work in progress even with me, let alone third parties, unless I bring the matter up first.

Where we get our ideas is at the heart of how we work and what we do. Trying to explain in rational, analytical fashion how we come up with our plots and our thematic structures threatens in an odd sort of way to reveal that we are all just humbugs hiding behind a velvet curtain. Better to let it all remain a mystery. Better to keep what little we can explain to ourselves.

All well and good, except that taking this tack suggests we are cowards, and the word *cowardly* might work once in a while for lions, but it is bad news for writers. If writers are afraid of something, they are supposed to work it out through their writing. They are supposed to confront the questions and the issues that disturb them. They are supposed to make sense of the larger world and its complexities.

So that is what I have decided to attempt here, to think back through the stories I have written and the ideas that prompted them. By examining a few, I hope to give you some insight into how the process works and where those mysterious ideas really come from.

Let me start with *The Wishsong of Shannara*. This is how that book came to be written. I was musing on the traditional Sirens of Greek mythology who lured unfortunate sailors to their doom. Odysseus only just missed becoming a victim. Such power! I began to wonder what it would do to you if by singing you could destroy things. Or create, perhaps. What if by singing you could change the way things were? What would you do with such power? What would such power do to you?

I took it a step further. Suppose there were siblings, and each had the power of a Siren. A sister and a brother would do. What if the sister could actually change things, but the brother could give only the appearance of change? But, wait! What if the former fell under the sway of her own magic, a victim of the very power she relied upon, and the latter, the weaker of the two, had to rise above his limitations and find a way to save her?

That was how Brin and Jair Ohmsford were conceived as the central figures in the book. The wishsong became an inherited trait, but a deadly one that could work both good and evil and was not always controllable by its users. Its magic, like the magic in all of my stories, was a two-edged sword that could cut either way. Brin and Jair would have to find a way to control it in order to save themselves.

Perhaps you are already seeing a pattern to what I do to

come up with ideas. I start asking questions. What if this? What if that? I ask these questions until I come to the central question of the whole exercise, and then either I find my story or I abandon the effort and start all over again. Sooner or later I find a set of questions that suggest a real story, and I am ready to put together a new book.

All right, let's try it again. This time let's delve a little deeper into the process. The book I am going to use is *Running with the Demon*. I began writing this book in 1996, after thinking on and off about the story for the better part of ten years. I hoped to accomplish several things. First, I wanted a dark, contemporary fantasy. Second, I wanted a book in which the story's magic fitted seamlessly with what we know to be true about the real world. Third, I wanted to write about growing up in a small town in the Midwest, and I particularly wanted to address the way in which children lose their beliefs about what is possible the more exposed they become to the world's harsh truths.

I mulled these elements over, searching for a storyline that would incorporate and address all three. Nothing worked. Then one day, while I was driving on the Seattle freeway, another driver cut me off in truly reckless fashion. It wasn't as if this hadn't happened before, but for some reason on that particular day it made me think about human behavior in the larger sense. I despaired that we had forsaken so many of the common courtesies. I bemoaned that we had forgotten how to be kind to each other in the way we were when the world was less complicated and hurried. I also worried that I was turning into my father, but I put that thought aside.

What I ended up wondering was whether we might be a people in the process of destroying ourselves without realizing it. Could our commonplace failures of consideration and caring be the harbinger of a larger social breakdown? Wasn't that how all civilizations eventually began to destroy themselves? Small cracks lead to large fissures, and the walls come tumbling down?

This was where the idea for *Running with the Demon* began. The what-if questions continued. What if our self-induced destruction was being aided and abetted by a truly dark force? What if that darkness was balanced by a force of light, and the two had been locked in battle since the dawn of time—a familiar concept. But here is the clincher. What if you were someone who knew this was happening and could do something about it; how much of yourself and your life would you be willing to sacrifice for the chance to make a difference?

From those questions emerged the characters of John Ross, the Knight of the Word, who is the paladin of hope for a world under siege from the forces of the Void, and Nest Freemark, the teenager whose dark family history hides a handful of secrets that could lead to the Knight's success or failure. More questions followed, each one leading to another, opening new doors and revealing fresh ideas. It works like that. In your thinking, you build your story one brick at a time until you have a recognizable house in which to move about. For *Running with the Demon*, the ideas came so fast and so easily that I could barely get one down on paper before another surfaced. Before I finished thinking about that book, I had the framework in place for two more. I had a trilogy with a beginning, a middle, and an ending book, a perfect circle to take the reader through three crucial meetings between the two main characters, each of which would prove to be life-transforming.

Where do you get your ideas? Mostly, from asking questions

and thinking about the answers. From considering possibilities and wondering to what they might lead. From letting your mind run free and taking a close look at whatever it happens to stumble across. It isn't thinking so much as it is dreaming. But all things begin with dreaming.

Lester del Rey told me repeatedly that the first and most important part of writing fiction is just to think about the story. Don't write anything down. Don't try to pull anything together right away. Just dream for a while and see what happens. There isn't any timetable involved, no measuring stick for how long it ought to take. For each book, it is different. But that period of thinking, of reflection, is crucial to how successful your story will turn out to be.

Here's another news flash for everyone who has ever asked a writer where he gets his ideas. Or she. Getting ideas is the least difficult part of the process. What's hard, really hard, is making those ideas come together in a well-conceived, compelling story. So many of those ideas that seem wonderful at first blush end up leading nowhere. They won't sustain the weight of a story. They won't spin out past a few pages. They won't lead to something insightful and true.

Ideas are like chocolates, as Forrest Gump might say. You never know what you are going to get.

I could have the idea on loan. He would give it to me for exactly one year. If I wrote an acceptable book in that time, the idea was mine to keep. Otherwise, I would have to give it back.

BLUEPRINT

IN LATE WINTER of 1984, I flew east from Sterling to New York City for a meeting with Lester del Rey. I made the trip for several reasons, but foremost of these was the desire to talk with him about what I would write next. Rewrites for *The Wishsong of Shannara* were complete, and it was time to consider a new project. I knew I did not want to do another *Shannara* book right away. After fifteen years of working in the *Shannara* world, I was burned out. I needed to write something else, but I did not know what that something else should be.

I had some ideas, of course. What writer doesn't? But I was leery of how they would be received. One year earlier, I presented a synopsis for a book entitled *The Koden King*, and both Lester and Judy-Lynn hated it. They did not say they hated it, not directly, but it was easy enough to read between the lines of their comments. They were encouraging of my work, as always, but clear about their opinion of the proposed book. I was tempted this time to call ahead to ask for guidance. I might not like what I heard, but at least I would avoid laying my neck on the chopping block right off the bat. But that was the coward's way out, so I decided to take my chances.

My confusion over where to go next was further complicated by the fact that I was at a crossroads in my life. I was an attorney in a small law firm and had been so for almost the same amount of time I had been writing *Shannara* books. I had become an attorney so that I would not starve to death trying to become a writer. But it had grown increasingly difficult to allocate my time between the two professions. Both were demanding; both really required all my energy, not just some of it. Seven years earlier, on the eve of publication of *The Sword of Shannara*, I made a bargain with myself that I would not consider myself a real writer until I had three books in print. Lester amended that bargain, on learning of it, by adding that I should also have a year's salary in the bank.

With the publication of *Wishsong*, I would have both. But I was still unsure about giving up my law practice. I know, I know. Was I waiting for a voice from a burning bush or something? But you have to remember how structured my life was back then. I was terrified of taking a wrong step. Practicing law provided a certain balance to my life that I was afraid I would miss badly if I gave it up. What if by abandoning law I knocked the pins out from under my writing? What if all that newly acquired time was too much time, and I found I could not write anything? What if I was not as ready as I thought?

So I came to New York and my meeting with Lester in search of more than just an idea for a new book. I came looking to discover the direction my life should take. I came seeking an epiphany.

On arrival, I checked into the Waldorf-Astoria hotel, which is where I always stayed in those days. It was close to Ballantine Books, which was located at the corner of East 50th Street and 2nd Avenue, and to the del Reys, who lived off 2nd on East 46th. Everyone was only a few blocks away, so I could walk to wherever I wanted to go. I knew I would spend most of the next day in a meeting with Lester at his apartment, then have dinner with both del Reys and one or two others a couple of blocks away at Sparks. I knew this because this is what we always did when I came to New York. Sometimes I thought Lester spent most of his time at home or at Sparks. With the passage of time, it became increasingly hard to picture him anywhere else.

I arrived late and slept in the following morning. Toward noon, I walked over to Lester's. The del Reys shared a cavernous loft apartment in what I think must have been a converted warehouse. The apartment was essentially one room, with a small bedroom leading off one end, a bathroom midway along, and a raised overlook that served as Lester's office and always reminded me of a pulpit. Lester and I sat in the living room portion of the apartment and ate a lunch of cold meats, cheese, and bread. We talked about *Wishsong*, about its publication, about other writers, about writing, about all the things that interest a writer and an editor. Everything but what I had really come to New York to talk about.

Finally, too impatient to wait longer, I brought the subject up. I wanted to do something besides another *Shannara* book, I told him. I was not leaving the series, only taking a vacation. But I needed to write something else. This was essentially what I had already told him over the phone before flying in. Lester agreed that writing something different might be a good idea. A writer needed to do more than one series anyway. What sort of book did I have in mind? I told him I wanted to do a fantasy, but not an epic fantasy. Something shorter, maybe lighter in tone. Something different. Something that would give me a break from the *Shannara* world.

I asked the crucial question. Did he have any ideas?

Not really, he responded at once, looking thoughtful. Oh, he had an idea for a story, all right. A good story, as a matter of fact. But I was not the right person to tell it.

I bristled at the implication. Why not?

Because it wasn't my kind of story, Lester responded. It wasn't my sort of book.

Well, how could he be sure of that? Perhaps it was. Tell me what it was about. Let me decide.

No, there wasn't any purpose in doing that, because it just wasn't the right story for me.

Tell me anyway, I insisted. Humor me. At least give me the plot. Maybe hearing about it would spark an idea I could use.

Lester sighed as only Lester could—long, drawn out, and reluctant. Then he told me his idea. The story was about a man who gets his hands on one of those high-end Christmas catalogues and while paging through it finds an advertisement for a magic kingdom. He decides to buy it, even though it doesn't seem possible that such a thing can exist. It turns out that it does, of course, but it also turns out that it isn't anything at all like what he imagined it would be.

Lester looked at me hopelessly, conveying the clear impression that the idea and I were not suited. I told him I liked it, that I thought maybe I could do something with it. I don't know why I said that. I didn't have the foggiest notion what I would do with it. But the gauntlet had been thrown down, and besides, something about the idea was appealing.

I like it, I told him. Really. Let me see what I can come up with.

He considered the matter for a few moments, then nodded. All right, I could have the idea on loan. He would give it to me for exactly one year. If I wrote an acceptable book in that time, the idea was mine to keep. Otherwise, I had to give it back.

On looking back after fifteen years, I am convinced that at that moment Lester looked a lot like Rumplestiltskin.

The fact of the matter was, I had been sucked in again. I didn't figure this out for quite a while, perhaps because I was obtuse, but more probably because I was so caught up in the challenge I didn't stop to think about how carefully it had been orchestrated. Later, as with so many other things, Lester told me that he had intended the idea for me all along, but felt I would respond better if he didn't hand it to me on a platter.

In any case, I completed my visit, took my borrowed idea, and flew home to Illinois. I was already thinking it through, trying to make it come together as a complete story. All I had was a concept, and a concept is just a starting point for expansion. A full-blown story requires a great deal more, and it is not a given that even the best idea can be successfully developed into a story that works.

I knew right away that the man who buys the magic kingdom would discover that it was not all it was cracked up to be. The old saw "The grass is always greener on the other side of the fence" would be tested anew. What the man thought he

was buying was not in fact what he would get. Nor would being a king of his own kingdom necessarily work out the way
he expected either. It would prove more difficult than he imagined. Obstacles he hadn't anticipated would arise. This is the
way life works. Even kings find that out sooner or later.

Then two questions surfaced, pretty much at the same time.

Who is this man?

Why is he buying this magic kingdom?

Everything else in the story hinged on the answers to these
two questions—where the story was going, how it would
resolve itself, and why the reader would identify with the
protagonist.

I was surprised at how quickly the answers came to me. I
discovered them almost immediately.

The man was a lawyer, and he was fed up with his life and
wanted to change it. He wanted to change it at any cost. He
was that desperate.

The man was me.

The revelation was stunning. I had lived all forty years of
my life in the same town, save for time spent going to college
and law school. I had been a lawyer for fifteen years, the last
seven of them compromising myself as a writer so that if I
failed, I would not sink into the mire and starve to death. I had
wanted to be a writer since I was ten, but I had never been just
a writer. I had never given myself the chance.

This was who the man in my book was. This was why he
was willing to risk everything to buy a dream.

I began work on the book almost at once. As I wrote it,
I talked about it now and then with Lester. In doing so, I discovered that he had envisioned a story more on the order
of a Piers Anthony *Xanth* novel, light and breezy, filled with

jokes and puns, a romp through an imaginary world that would cause readers to smile.

But I saw the story in a darker light. As a writer, I am drawn to harder-edged issues, particularly those dealing with life-altering decisions and secrets that destroy. So even though I cloaked this book in trappings of humor and populated it with peculiar and sometimes comical characters, the questions I asked were serious. What happens when you change your life completely? What are the consequences of abandoning everything you know? What is the impact on you and those around you when things do not work out as you expect?

I wrote the book in a little over ten months. It is the story of Ben Holiday, a Chicago trial attorney who loses his wife and baby in an auto accident, grows frustrated with a legal system he sees as antiquated and unfair, and searches for a way to change his life. When he comes across an advertisement in a high-end Christmas catalogue that lists a magic kingdom for sale for one million dollars, he is intrigued. On something of a lark and out of desperation, he decides to look into it. He flies to New York to interview for the position of king of Landover with an old man named Meeks (who looks and acts a lot like Lester). He ends up buying the kingdom and arrives through a curtain of mist in the Blue Ridge Mountains of Virginia. But being king isn't what he expected. His friends and retainers include a bumbling wizard with mixed intentions, a man who has been turned into a dog and can't change back, two kobolds of uncertain temperament, and a young sylph who regularly morphs into a tree. He also discovers that his alter ego in Landover is a ferocious, silent black knight who lives only to do combat and whose secret he must unmask if he is to survive.

Lester liked the book well enough that he let me keep the

idea. I called it *Holiday's Magic*. Lester promptly changed the title to *Magic Kingdom for Sale*. He scheduled it for publication in April of 1986.

I didn't recognize the book for what it was until I went on a book tour to promote it. What I had written was a blueprint for my life. I couldn't foresee all the consequences yet, but I could guess at most of them, good and bad. The die was cast. A part-time writer for more than thirty years, I owed it to myself to try writing full-time, to give myself the chance to discover if I could make a living doing what I loved most.

I returned to Sterling and quit my job. I moved to Seattle. I began my new life. It wasn't always easy; there were many complications. But overall, it felt right. In time, I discovered that it was right.

In time-honored fashion, life had imitated art. To my surprise, my book did not lead me into the wilderness after all.

Instead, it led me home.

The list of successful authors who claim not to
outline their books before they write them goes
on and on. All right, you say, so why are you
telling us we should outline when they don't?

THE DREADED "O" WORD

N OW WE COME to the two chapters that are certain to be the most controversial. I have pushed them as far back into the book as I can, hoping that if you have gotten this far in your reading, you will stick it out for another few pages. This chapter and the next are intended primarily for unpublished writers looking to become published, but I'm hoping readers in general will find them interesting, too.

Sue Grafton would title this first chapter in her writing manual, if she had one, "O Is for Outline."

I have a very simple ten-word formula for success as a writer of long fiction. It might apply to all forms of writing, but my experience is primarily in writing long fiction, so I am limiting the application of the formula to that form alone. I give this formula to you, as I do to anyone I speak to about writing, free of charge. It goes like this:

Read, Read, Read.
Outline, Outline, Outline.
Write, Write, Write.
Repeat.

I don't get much argument about steps one and three, which are pretty much self-evident to anyone with real aspirations for becoming a published writer. Nor does anyone have too much to say about step four, which is difficult to avoid in this business unless the degree of luck you experience in attempting to interest a publisher in your work is legendary.

But whole bunches of people recoil with genuine horror when I mention step two. They remember with no fondness whatsoever their secondary school experiences. They remember what they had to go through in learning about outlining from one or more teachers of English. The hated words still echo somewhere in the deep recesses of their minds. *Large Roman Numeral One, Capital A, small Roman numeral one, little a*—a litany of senseless conformity and rote invented solely to drive students mad.

Well, forget all that. When I speak of outlining, I want you to think of something else entirely, something that shares only one thing in common with all that early secondary school nonsense. That one thing is another "O" word—organization.

Now, you are going to hear a lot of very successful writers tell you that they don't outline their books. Never have, never will. They are going to give you all sorts of reasons why you shouldn't either—sometimes in direct fashion, sometimes by implication. *I've never done it,* they will advise, *so it's all right if you don't.* Or, *I've never seen the point to it, so how could you?* Like that. I've listened to and read comments like this for years—not from writers selling five thousand copies of their books a year, but five hundred thousand.

Let me give you some examples. Stephen King writes in his entertaining and informative book *On Writing* that plotting just gets in the way of storytelling and robs it of its spontaneity. He prefers just to plop down characters in a challenging situation and see what they will do. Anne Lamott in her wonderful book on what it is like to become a published writer, *Bird by Bird,* talks about just sitting down at the keyboard with no plan in mind whatsoever and thrashing around for hours, sometimes days, until something finally happens. I've listened to Terry McMillan, on being asked about outlining, reply to an audience of two thousand at the Maui Writers Conference, "Why would I want to tell the same story twice?" On a fantasy writing panel several years ago, after I had given my usual spiel about the importance of outlining, I had Anne McCaffrey turn to me and gently and sweetly say, "Terry, I don't think I've ever outlined anything in my life."

The list of successful writers who claim not to outline their books before they write them goes on and on. All right, you say, so why are you telling us we should outline when they don't? Why can't we do like they do? Why can't we just sit down and tell our stories?

Well, maybe you can. Maybe you're one of the lucky ones who can make it work. On the other hand, maybe not. We know right off the bat that you probably aren't Stephen King or Anne Lamott or Terry McMillan or Anne McCaffrey. We also know that a lot of other writers aren't either, and a fair number, some of them very successful, do outline their work before they sit down to write their books.

Ask yourself this: How many books have you read where the author introduced a plot element that seemed to never go anywhere? Or involved you with a character who wandered off somewhere along the way and never returned? How many books have you read where the first three hundred pages were wonderful, and then everything fell apart—where you had the feeling that the author was just looking to wrap things up and get paid? How many books have you read that were so disjointed in their storytelling that you had to keep looking back to see where they were going? How many books have you read that were so empty of purpose that by the time you finished reading them—supposing you got that far—you felt you had been cheated out of the twenty-five-dollar purchase price?

I would suggest that all of these problems are organizational in nature, which means it is more likely than not that the author failed to do a lick of outlining.

Writing isn't a crapshoot. Publishing, yes—but not writing. Writing is a craft. You can learn it, and you can learn to do it better. As you've already read previously in this book, you might have it in you to be a writer or you might not; that's just the way it is. But if you do have it in you, what you would like to do is to reduce the odds of producing a piece of writing that doesn't represent your best effort.

So let me give you my thoughts on why I think outlining is a valuable tool that doesn't have to deflate your excitement before you even get started or turn your writing experience into a boring exercise in word assembly.

If you outline your book in advance, you will force yourself to think your story through. To some degree, depending on how thorough you choose to be, you will have to juggle plot, characters, settings, points of view, and thematic structure in order to assemble your story. You will have to build a story arc—a beginning, middle, and end—that comprises the gist of your book. You will have to consider all the possible choices you can imagine in crucial situations and select the ones that seem best. You won't do this for every twist and turn the book takes, but you will do it for the big ones. You will take this information and you will write it down in some recognizable fashion so that you can refer to it later.

This accomplishes several important goals.

It gives you a working blueprint to which you can refer later. Now, I don't know about you, but it takes me a while to write a book. It doesn't take just days or weeks, but months and sometimes years. For me, that's a long time to remember stuff. After fifty-odd years of dealing with life's vicissitudes, I find I don't remember things as well as I used to—or maybe as well as I think I used to. Having written down what it was you intended to do and where it was you intended to go can be a big help. Five months after you've started a book, you can still look at that blueprint and know what it was you wanted to accomplish when you started out—not only with the story at large, but with every major plot point and character.

By having outlined, you are also in a better position to know during the course of your writing when you are being scammed by trickster plot twists and duplicitous characters— by all those ideas that seem so good at the time, but in the end will lead you astray. It is a given that in the writing of any book, your outline will change. I mean, come on, you didn't think I was going to tell you your outline was written in stone, did you? These are working drawings we're talking about. These are sketches. Nothing informs the writer about how a book should come together like the actual writing of it. Remember what I said earlier about discarding all those preconceived notions about outlines? Here's a good place to start. No matter how thoroughly or carefully you have considered your story, you are going to get new and better ideas about how it should be told when you actually write it. You are going to see places where you can improve on the original plot, tighten the narrative, better use a character, and so on and so forth.

But by having already considered most of the possibilities while you were constructing your outline, you can now make a more informed decision about which way to go. Because you have those working drawings at hand, you can tell how a change you are contemplating will impact the rest of your book. The end result is that you can do a better job of keeping at bay those plot lines and characters that will play you false.

I would also argue that there is a good chance that an outline will help you stave off any onslaught of writer's block. Let me advise you right up front that I am not a big believer in writer's block. I think writer's block is God's way of telling you one of two things—that you failed to think your material through sufficiently before you started writing, or that you need a day or two off with your family and friends. In the latter instance, God frequently speaks to me through Judine. In the former, listen to this voice of reason as it whispers in your ear. *Hssst! If you want to avoid writing yourself into the box of dead ends or out into the desert of poor ideas or off into the wilderness of ill-considered plot choices, an outline will help!*

Perhaps the best reason of all for outlining is that it frees you up immeasurably during the writing process to concentrate on matters other than plot. Think about it. Each chapter needs to be told from a character's point of view, needs to establish a mood and set a scene, likely requires both narrative and dialogue, and probably demands a sense of movement. That's just the bare bones of it, but even that much is fairly daunting. Plus, you have to think about how your story will come across to the reader. What words and images will you use? What emotions will you try to evoke? Where is the conflict in this scene? Is there a turning point, a secret, a revelation, a red herring?

Now, on top of that you want to mess around with trying to figure out your plot? Who do you think you are—Houdini?

Okay, I exaggerate. I'm a writer, what do you expect? But the core truth remains unaltered. If you take time in the beginning to think your story through and commit some of those thoughts to paper in the form of an outline, you will free yourself up later to concentrate on other matters of writing and thereby reduce some of the stress in your life.

In the next chapter, we'll take a look at specific ways in which you can make this process work.

Just sitting down and thinking about writing doesn't always work. It would be nice if it did, but the creative process is more complicated than simply deciding to create and then doing it.

DREAM TIME

LET ME BEGIN by repeating that you need to forget
all about the kind of outlining you were taught in grammar and English classes as a kid. Forget about Roman Numeral One and Capital A. Forget about the whole idea of a
structure comprised of neatly numbered and indented para-
graphs. We don't want that approach. We don't want anything
remotely like it. We want organization, but not conformity or
rigidity.

I'm going to use my own approach as a working model. I'm
not saying you should do things exactly the same way I do. For
each of us, the approach to outlining a book is going to vary,
just like our approach to writing. That's all right. You want to

find a way that will work for you. By offering my approach as an example, I'm hoping you can figure out your own.

For me, it begins with just thinking about what I want to write—the plot, characters, setting, mood, pacing, point of view, twists and turns, thematic structure, anything and everything that has to do with the story. I have learned it is a process I cannot rush. Sometimes it goes quickly and sometimes it takes forever. Think of it as a percolation period, when you let your ideas brew and the flavor of your story build.

Lots of ideas occur to me while this is going on. I don't write them down. I don't write anything down—except for names, which go on a name list I carry with me everywhere. But nothing else. It's a firm rule. I used to think that if I got an idea, I should write it down immediately so that I wouldn't lose it. Sometimes I would wake in the middle of the night with brilliant ideas that I would dash down on slips of paper so they would be saved for when I awoke the next morning. What happened was that either I couldn't make sense of them or they turned out to be not so brilliant after all. So I've changed my thinking on this. If an idea doesn't stick with me for more than twenty-four hours, it probably wasn't all that hot in the first place.

Anyway, this thinking period—this dream time—is crucial to everything that happens later, but particularly to the construction of my outline. I want to be able to picture my story in images before I try to reduce it to mere words. I want to think about the possibilities. Everyone asks a writer where he gets his ideas. You've already seen the chapter on that. The truth is that coming up with ideas is easy; it's making up the stories that grow out of them that's hard.

Sometimes I have to jump-start the process. Just sitting

down and thinking about writing doesn't always work. It would be nice if it did, but the creative process is more complicated than simply deciding to create and then doing it. Sometimes, my mind doesn't like it when I try to put it to work, and it just shuts down. Sometimes, it chooses to think about other things. Instead of focusing on how I can solve that latest plot dilemma, it prefers to concentrate on how long it will be until I eat again or whether or not the sprinkler system will stick on for another twenty-four hours like it did yesterday. Trying to tell it what to do is like trying to teach your cat to sit up and beg. If it feels like it, it will. If it doesn't, good luck.

What I can do to banish that recalcitrant attitude is to put myself in an atmosphere that encourages dreaming. Some moods and settings and experiences are more conducive to creative thinking than others. For each of us, this varies. I find I am able to free up my thinking best in a couple of very specific ways.

One is to take a long drive, preferably out in the country somewhere. Driving puts me in a zone that allows me to concentrate on the mechanics of driving the car while thinking of something else entirely. I find myself coming up with ideas I could never imagine if I just sat down and tried to conjure them. Maybe it's the movement, but it works every time.

A second freeing experience is to go to the symphony. I can sit there listening to the music and disappear into another world. I don't know why, but classical music seems to suggest fresh places and new stories. It transports me. It causes me to imagine possibilities for writing that invariably yield something good. This result doesn't come about with any other kind of music. When I was a kid, I used to do the same thing using stirring sound tracks from movies like *Ivanhoe* and

Plymouth Adventure. Now, it's classical music. I'd like to think my tastes have matured, but I'm afraid the truth is otherwise.

In any case, listening to classical music and taking long drives are what work for me. You will have to find out what works for you. But something will. Something will help free up your creative thinking and allow you to start imagining the possibilities.

But enough about you. Let's get back to me. At some point, the mass of images floating around in my head reaches critical mass, and I have to get them out of there. That's when it's time to write them all down on paper. I don't have to put them down in any particular order or with any specific plan in mind. They just need to be recorded, all of them, for a more balanced consideration of what they might lead to. By now, I probably have a pretty good idea of what the new book is going to be about. Some of my images will be fully formed. I will fill pages and pages of yellow tablets with handwritten notes. This usually takes a couple of weeks, but it can go faster. While I am writing, new ideas will occur, and I will add them to the mix. I am done when I can't think of anything else to write down.

Now I have a collection of plotlines, character sketches, and thematic developments both large and small. Some of these will get used, some will get set aside for another story, and some will get tossed out altogether. The trick is in separating them into the right piles. A lot of this is simply gut instinct, but there are two ironclad rules I have come to rely on.

The first rule is that nothing goes into one of my books that isn't grounded in something real and true about the human condition. Sure, I write fantasy. But I learned years ago from Lester del Rey that the secret to writing good fantasy is to make certain it relates to what we know about our own world. Readers must be able to identify with the material in such a way that they recognize and believe the core truths of the storytelling. It doesn't matter if you are writing epic fantasy, contemporary fantasy, dark urban fantasy, comic fantasy, cookbook fantasy, or something else altogether, there has to be truth in the material. Otherwise, readers are going to have a tough time suspending disbelief long enough to stay interested.

The second rule is that everything I include must advance the story in some measurable way. There are lots of clever ideas, colorful characters, and wondrous plot twists lurking around in your head, demanding attention, seeking a place in your books. Unless they do something to further the development of your story, unless they serve a purpose, get rid of them. If all they do is take up space and look cute, get them out of there. Think of them as annoying phone solicitors who interrupt your writing time. They might have something good to sell and they might be fun to talk to, but they aren't going to do a thing for your career. Tell them you will take their names and call them back. Maybe when you are done writing this book, you will have a place for them in the next.

The last step in this process is to pull everything together into a story arc with a beginning, middle, and end—in short, where the story starts, where it goes, and how it concludes. I don't need to know everything. But I do need to have the big picture in mind, and I do need a clear idea of how I am going to go about painting it.

Several written exercises will help me achieve this. The most important of these is a chapter-by-chapter breakdown of the book. Each chapter can be covered in no more than a paragraph or two that records the essential elements of who, what, and where. If there are particular considerations, I make note of them. The writing itself will determine whether these thumbnails stay in their original form or change. What is important is that I end up with a structure I can use to help keep everything straight.

I also like to make up sketches of the main characters. The size of these will vary. A physical description will be included, but there might also be a mention of strengths or flaws or even of particular ways in which I want the character to impact the story. I like to know how these characters will interact and when. I like to project ways in which they will change over the course of the book.

I will also frequently write several pages of description of an important setting. Sometimes this is a composite of what I've really seen and what I've imagined. It will include physical descriptions of how things taste and smell. It will advise if there are trees or houses or lakes or mountains, if it is a wilderness or a settled area, if it is hot or cold, wet or dry, hospitable or savage. Mostly, it will provide me with a way to immerse myself in the surroundings of my characters so that when I begin to write about them, I will know how they feel about their world.

You may have noticed by now that the common denominator in all this is dreaming. It is imagining how things will be before writing them down. It is seeing them in my mind and making certain that my vision of them is clear. It is picking and choosing, keeping and discarding, and above all, organizing. Much of it will never appear in the book. Much of it will prove to be superfluous to the story itself—deep background, which only the author needs to know. But all of it will keep me honest. It will inform my writing and provide the reader with a sense of confidence in my storytelling.

Of course, doing all this requires a lot of hard work, which is one very definite reason some writers steer clear of the outlining process entirely. Sure, the dreaming part is fun and freeing, but the organizing and writing down of plotlines and themes is tough business. It's much easier to forget all that and just sit down and start writing and see what happens. But if you check what most writers who don't outline have to say about their work habits, you will discover that they end up doing several drafts of a book and any number of rewrites afterwards.

I don't. I do one draft, one rewrite, and I'm done.

Is this because I'm a better writer than they are? In my dreams. No, it has to do with how you want to allocate your workload. The truth is simple. You can either do the hard work up front or do it at the end. By outlining, you are doing the hard work in the beginning—the thinking, the organizing, the weighing and considering, and the making of choices. By doing it early, you can save yourself a lot of time and effort at the end. Put it off, and you pay the price later. Writing requires a certain amount of suffering for the pleasure it gives back. Nothing you do will ever change that. But you can help yourself by distributing the load.

None of this is to say that by outlining you have eliminated the need for creative thinking during the actual writing process. What you have done is lay the groundwork. Writing the book will dictate the need for changes in your thinking. It will provide fresh insights into how the story needs to unfold. It will require new and better approaches to plot points you had earlier believed were good enough. But, gosh, look what you've got that other writers don't! You've got a blueprint to refer to. You've got a way to determine how those changes and insights and ideas will impact the rest of your book, and you can make sure that the impact is a positive one.

Moreover, you've freed yourself up to concentrate on the writing process itself, on the telling of the story, together with all its complex demands and mechanics. You don't have to burden yourself with also trying to figure out what is going to happen every step of the way. Sure, sometimes your plot comes easily enough. You just know what you're meant to do, and you do it. But lots of times it doesn't work that way. Lots of times it's tough sledding. You can grease your runners up a little bit by trying what I suggest and doing some of the hardest work up front. You can think your plot through before you start to write about it.

Lester del Rey used to tell me that thinking about a book before you wrote it was as important as the writing itself. Too many authors, he opined, just rushed right into their story without giving a thought to what they were doing. The result was a lot of very bad books and a lot of hard work for editors who had to try to fix them. At the time, I thought he was just being curmudgeonly. Now, I think he was being insightful.

A few years back, I started sending pictures of myself stretched out on a lounge chair, lying on a beach, eyes closed, soaking up the sun. I backed them on postcards that included a message that read something like "This is me at work." It was meant as a joke, of course, but the truth is that this is exactly how a writer does some of his most important work. Dreaming opens the doors to creativity. Dreaming allows the imagination to invent something wonderful. Don't cheat yourself out of a chance to discover how well this can work. Don't shortcut the process.

Make dream time the linchpin of your writing experience. Start right now. Put down this book. Find a lounge chair and lie down and close your eyes. Let your mind drift.

Go some place you've never been, then come back and tell us all about it.

I told him what I wanted. He told me in response

and in no uncertain terms that I was crazy.

I had no idea what I was getting myself into.

HOOK

I WAS SITTING with Judine in a café in Albuquerque's Old Town in the spring of 1991 when I made one of the worst decisions of my life. It was midday on a Sunday, the weather clear and hot and dry, and the plaza outside the café filled with shoppers and sightseers. I was in the middle of a book tour and had nothing to do until a book event at two that afternoon at a store called Page One. Judine and I had come to Old Town to eat New Mexican food and drink margaritas, and we had done plenty of both.

Because I was feeling so good about things, I decided to call Owen Lock. Owen had been editor in chief at Del Rey Books since Judy-Lynn's death in 1986. He was also my friend.

Owen came to Del Rey as Judy-Lynn's assistant about the same time that *The Sword of Shannara* showed up on her doorstep, so we had sort of grown up together in the company. I reached Owen at home, and we talked about how the tour was going, what the weather was like, how Lester seemed with Judy-Lynn gone, and so on and so forth.

Then, just before hanging up, he mentioned a piece of good news. Del Rey Books had bought the rights to the book tie-in to a new Steven Spielberg movie called *Hook*, which was intended as a sequel to J. M. Barrie's *Peter Pan*. Robin Williams would play Peter, who has finally grown up, and Dustin Hoffman would play Captain Hook, who has not. The movie should be a huge success, Owen said, so Del Rey was gearing up for doing the book adaptation and a series of spin-offs on related subjects. What they needed to do right now was to find a writer for the adaptation. He would let me know whom they selected.

He hung up, and I went back to Judine to tell her the news. While sipping another margarita, I contemplated the prospect of a sequel to *Peter Pan*. It seemed a truly inspired idea. I was in love with it. More to the point, I wanted to do the book. After all, who better to write a sequel to *Peter Pan* than me, the boy who never grew up? Why should this project go to someone else when I was the best writer available? I was infused with sudden purpose. I had to write this book. I knew I could do it. I knew I could do it better than anyone.

I told Judine of my feelings. She knew me too well even then to argue the matter. Instead, she told me that if I felt so strongly about it, I should call Owen back. So I did. I told him what I wanted. He told me in response and in no uncertain terms that I was crazy. I had no idea what I was getting myself into. I persisted nevertheless. Had he seen the script? Yes. Was it wonderful? Yes. Did it follow the tenor and line of the original? Yes. If I wanted to do it, would the publisher let me? A long, heartfelt sigh ensued through the telephone receiver. They would love for you to do it, he admitted. But you won't get paid anything, and you will live to regret the whole business. Movie people are not like us. They are not like anyone. Listen to what I am saying. Give it up.

But I didn't listen to him and I didn't give it up. I was enamored of the idea of writing the sequel to *Peter Pan*, even if what I was doing was only an adaptation of somebody else's work. I could shape it to my own vision, I told myself. I could embellish it with my own style. It would be wonderful, especially with a movie starring Robin Williams and Dustin Hoffman to help publicize it.

Thus did I run swiftly and foolishly to my doom.

When I got home, I spoke with Susan Petersen, then president of Ballantine Books, and told her what I wanted to do. She thought it was a wonderful idea. We quickly came to an agreement regarding advances and royalties against earnings. I was so eager to do this project that I paid almost no attention to any of the financial details. What was important was the opportunity to (a) write in the world of James Barrie and (b) attract the attention of new readers for my other books. I was sent a copy of the movie script, which I read and loved. The script, by Jim V. Hart, was true to the original story of *Peter Pan* and very inventive. I could hardly wait to start work. All that remained was a quick trip to Hollywood to visit the sets and talk with the Spielberg people (perhaps, if I was lucky, Steven Spielberg himself or one of the movie stars).

Matters started to deteriorate from there.

I asked if I could speak with the screenwriter, to get an

idea of his vision for the script, and was advised that he was no longer involved with the project. The script was already under revision. That would be the same script that I found so wonderful, I thought. The first faint rumblings of uncertainty surfaced like poisonous gas, but I ignored them.

The night before I was to fly to Los Angeles for a visit to the movie set was the last happy moment I would experience on this project until well after it was finished. On that night, I still had expectations of something good coming out of it.

Judine and I had arranged to fly down and back on the same day. We would visit the sets, discuss the script, and obtain help with the details necessary to enable me to write the book. That was what we thought, at least.

The reality proved to be somewhat different. When we arrived, we were driven to a trailer on the set and met by a midlevel functionary who clearly had better and more important things to do with his time than mess around with us. He told me right off the bat that we wouldn't be meeting Steven Spielberg or any of the stars. Well, maybe a Lost Boy or two. Nor would we be allowed to visit any of the sets except for one. They were all closed to visitors or already dismantled. The one that was available was of the Lost Boy camp in Never Never Land. A bit dismayed, I agreed to accept the crumb that was being offered.

We went to the one set we were allowed on. It was surprisingly small, about the size of a big toy assembly on a playground. I studied it dutifully, made some notes, and then asked if I might take a few pictures. Certainly not, our escort declared. No pictures allowed. I nodded meekly. No telling what I might do with those pictures.

We returned to the trailer. I asked if there were any pictures of the settings or scenes or characters I could look at. Our escort produced a small set of perhaps half a dozen color photos and a somewhat larger set of pen-and-inks. They were useful, but there were not nearly enough of them. I asked if he had any other pictures or drawings that I could see. He didn't. I asked if he could send me some later. He said he would let me know. I asked if I could take what he had shown me or make copies. He said no. He would check to see if I could have copies later. I would have to sign a confidentiality agreement, of course.

I flew home in a funk. Judine, wisely, said nothing. I called up Ellen Key Harris, my editor at Del Rey for the project, and asked for help. She said she would see what she could do. By now I realized that this was going to be everyone's favorite response on this project. I sat and waited. One week. Two. Three. Finally, out of sheer frustration, I began writing anyway, blocking out scenes and describing places and characters as best I could. I called Ellen and told her that I was writing the book and I certainly hoped it turned out to resemble in some small way the movie it was supposed to be based on, but if it didn't, too bad, I was out of patience and through waiting.

Within three days, a passel of pictures and drawings arrived—along with the ubiquitous confidentiality agreement, which I signed and returned.

Then things began to get really weird. In the first place, the story opened with a Little League baseball game being played at Christmastime with umpires dressed as Santa Clauses. The scene involved Peter, who had forgotten who he was, and his son, who was a member of the team. The important thing to know is that the scene took place in New York City in December.

Now, even I know they don't play baseball in New York City in the winter. So I called to ask about this. Oh, that's been changed, I was advised. The scene now takes place in Denver.

Denver? Winter baseball in Denver?

Before I could figure out what to do next, the scene was gone, replaced by a Christmas pageant about *Peter Pan*. But it was the beginning of a disturbing trend that would haunt me for the remainder of the time I worked on the book. Movie scenes, it seems, are not shot in order. They are shot on a schedule that has to do with locations, actor availability, and weather conditions. Worse, if the director decides he doesn't like a scene he has already shot, he might go back and shoot it over entirely.

Which was what was taking place while I was trying to write the book. Scenes were summarily dropped or reshot, with fresh script pages arriving almost daily. I tried to work around this, but it became an organizational nightmare. Scenes that were formerly dropped would suddenly be put back in again. Scenes that were changed were suddenly changed back. I quickly learned to throw nothing away because today's garbage might well be tomorrow's treasure. The movie was lurching all over the place, and I was lurching right along with it, trying desperately to keep the book consistent and the narrative tightly woven. It was like herding cats.

Finally, the whole business ground to a conclusion. The movie was finished, the editing completed, the rewrites and reshoots over. The original script had disappeared as a recognizable whole, replaced by a series of cobbled-together parts that were truly scary. But I had done what I could and I was satisfied that the book worked. Enough was enough.

I turned the manuscript in and thought I was out of the

woods. I was sadly mistaken, as Owen could have told me, had he deigned to bother.

Back came the manuscript with not one, not two, but three sets of rewrites from three separate movie people. I didn't know any of them and had no idea what their connection was with the Spielberg company. What I did know, after a quick reading of all three, was that they did not agree on any of the changes they had suggested. In fact, in many places, they were in direct contradiction.

Incensed, I called Ellen and used several four-letter words and a good deal of heat to describe how I felt about this whole business. I would not change one word of anything until there was some agreement between the people on the other end. In a huff, I sat down to wait once more.

The response, when it came, was truly bizarre. Without any explanation as to whom the three commentators were, I was told the following about each. Number One was a person of no consequence, just someone the movie company was trying to placate and whom I could ignore completely. Number Two was someone I should pay attention to, but whose suggestions I did not need to follow unless I chose to do so. Number Three was the only person who counted, and I must do as she ordered.

Fine. I tossed out comments from Numbers One and Two without another moment's consideration, thinking that the problem was solved. It was not. Number Three, whoever she was, had clearly never been involved in editing and perhaps never even read a book. A sample of her suggestions went like this. For a sentence that might read, "The room was night-black," the comment would be, "This action does not take place at night." For a sentence that might read, "It was as quiet as the sanctuary of a church," the comment would read, "The setting is the Lost Boys' hideout, not a church." A reference to Mickey Mouse brought a cryptic, "Delete all references to Disney characters."

I am not making this up, as Dave Barry would say.

Editing *Hook* became something akin to pulling teeth. I just went along with most of it, preferring not to get bogged down in the details. It was easier to delete than to argue. Those pages where I could not morally and reasonably give in, I handed over to Ellen to resolve, which she mostly did. In the end, it all got ironed out, and I refused all phone calls from Owen for a month.

I had already decided I would never do this again. It got worse, of course. My name could not appear on the cover of the book in larger type than those of the screenwriters. There was to be no mention inside of my other work. I was not to talk about the book until the movie was out. When the movie opened, I did not get free tickets from the studio. I stood in line at the box office and bought them like everyone else. I never heard from Steven Spielberg or the studio about what they thought of my work. In fact, I never heard another word about the book from anyone involved in the movie ever again.

The movie opened to mixed reviews and never lived up to expectations. The book did moderately well, but not well enough to make anyone forget sliced bread. It didn't do a thing for me as a writer. I had learned a hard lesson, but I had learned it thoroughly. When I finally accepted a call from Owen, I told him this: No more movie adaptations for me.

I repeated this litany for the next eight years at every book event where I was asked about movie tie-ins. Never again, I announced fiercely.

The reader wants to see something happen

between pages one and four hundred, and nothing

happens if the characters don't change.

MAUD MANX,
PART ONE

OKAY, IT'S TIME for some fun.

Not that we haven't been having plenty up until now, of course. But all this talk about craft can be pretty dry in the absence of examples that remind us that writing should always be, first and foremost, enjoyable.

I have some rules about writing that I follow rather rigorously, and this seems a good place to talk about them. They don't mean much outside of their practical application, so I thought I would give you a look at the way I might use them in my writing. But I don't want to tackle this task with anything serious and certainly not with one of my own books (Do you think I'm nuts?) so I have invented a story that I hope will illustrate the importance of my rules without putting you to sleep.

Let's pretend that I have decided to write a thriller. I've finished my dream time and come up with a fairly typical sort of tale. It involves a retired government operative, once the best in the business, who has been hunted down by her lifelong nemesis and now faces one final confrontation before she goes to that big CIA complex in the sky. This will be a classic kind of story, the hero alone against impossible odds, her courage and strength of character tested as she discovers that you can never really escape your past.

My lead character is Maud Manx, a real road warrior. At eighty years of age, she has slowed down a bit. She has only one arm, loves cats, hates birds, and once worked as a bookseller for a small independent bookstore specializing in books on plants and animals. She was with the CIA for thirty years, but has been retired for the past fifteen in the little town of Octogenarian, Montana, where she lives up in the mountains in a small cabin with her aging toms, Kibbles and Bits.

Her enemy is a ruthless scientist named Feral Finch. Finch was a CIA operative, as well, but he turned rogue and eventually formed his own network of troublemakers who have plagued the CIA ever since. Maud and Finch were once partners, but now are bitter enemies. Finch, in an experiment gone horribly wrong, turned himself from a man into a large bird and is unable to regain his human form. Embittered and vengeful, he blames the government (well, who doesn't?) for his problems. He also blames Maud. In an earlier confrontation, Finch, in his bird form, took off Maud's arm at the shoulder.

They haven't done battle in twenty years, but now Finch has come in search of Maud with the intent of doing her in. Alone and seemingly unprotected, her association with the

CIA long since ended, her strength depleted with age, and her skills dissipated by the passing of time, Maud must face her enemy alone.

Supporting characters include a small group of people that our mountain-dwelling retiree has come to know in the natural course of things. We have Alfred Stamp, the postman, who is known for his uncertain temper and erratic behavior; little Johnny Gazette, the paperboy, who sometimes brings Maud canned beets from his mother; and Martha Handy, the strange old lady who lives deep in the woods behind Maud and makes all her own clothes out of tree bark. I am also thinking about a local law enforcement presence, but haven't decided about that yet.

The title of my imaginary tome is *Cat Chaser*.

Pretty good so far, right? A catchy title, the promise of lots of excitement, a hero and villain who might prove interesting, and some potentially quirky supporting characters. Sure, it's silly and the only ones who could do it justice would be Dave Barry or Carl Hiaasen, but it will serve our purposes well enough.

So with our Maud Manx thriller as a working model, let's look at a few of those rules I mentioned earlier.

The first is a familiar one: WRITE WHAT YOU KNOW.

What the heck does that mean, anyway? Does it mean I can't write about anything that hasn't happened to me? If it doesn't involve the Midwest or lawyers or writers or bookselling, am I out of my depth? I've had lots of cats and dogs, so I'm on solid ground there, but I've never had much use for birds. I don't know anyone who has lost an arm. I've never worked for the CIA, though some of my editor's most successful authors are former spooks. So how am I supposed to follow this rule, given my limited life experience?

The answer, of course, is that this rule is not to be interpreted literally. I have heard E. L. Doctorow say that any writer of fiction should be able to write about any period in history after reading only a single sentence written from that time. He was telling his audience that writers are blessed with active imaginations for a reason. I need only enough familiarity with my subject matter to give the reader the *feeling* that I have some idea of what I am talking about. I don't need to know all about the CIA to write this story. I'm not writing about the CIA. By the same token, I don't need to have lost an arm to write about it. I just need to give my readers a sense of what that would be like, to make it feel real for them.

You can achieve most of what you need through a little bit of research, a smidgen of intuition, and a judicious use of imagination. What you want to avoid—what the rule is really all about—is trying to write a story in which the central elements rely on extensive life knowledge that you don't have. So, for example, you don't want to tackle a story in which the lead character is a doctor trying to cure cancer and where a consideration of various current advances in medicine is central to the plot if you don't know anything about doctors or cancer or medicine and don't want to research all three extensively. You want to write about aspects of the human condition that you are comfortable exploring or inhabiting over the course of your book.

If I want to make Maud and Feral former CIA operatives, I had better have a talk with my editor about what this is like and do some reading by some of those former spooks. It wouldn't hurt for me to do a little reading about people with disabilities, either.

This brings us to rule number two: YOUR CHARACTERS MUST BEHAVE IN A BELIEVABLE FASHION.

This rule is an important addendum to the first. If you don't know what you are writing about to begin with, it becomes difficult for you to know how to describe your characters. How do CIA operatives behave? How do they think? What makes them different from, say, policemen? Or are they? Even if you don't have life experience in this field, you have to find out, if you are going to make your protagonist believable.

It is important to understand that this doesn't mean that Maud can't do some things that are entirely out of character with what you discover to be true about CIA operatives or about her personally. But it does mean that what she does at any given point has to feel right in the context of the storytelling. She might well do something totally out of character, like offer help to a bird she finds lying injured by the side of the road, even though she hates birds. But I have to give the reader a reason to believe that she might behave in this way under the circumstances.

The meshing of your characters and your plot should feel seamless to the reader. It isn't inappropriate to let the reader wonder about how a character behaves at any given point, if somewhere down the road an explanation is offered or implied that brings everything back into line. What doesn't work is when a character acts in an offhanded, arbitrary way and no reason is ever given for this. Or worse, if a character behaves in a fashion that suggests the writer is attempting to solve a troublesome plot device with an easy out: the dreaded deus ex machina. Irrational or inconsistent behavior merely detracts from the effort at creating a wholly realized, believable character.

So in our development of Maud and Finch, we need to see them interact and react in ways that make sense to us in terms of what we know to be true about the larger world and the human condition.

The third rule is an easy one: A PROTAGONIST MUST BE CHAL-
LENGED BY A CONFLICT THAT REQUIRES RESOLUTION.

That's easy enough here, where Maud is facing a life-
threatening confrontation with an old enemy. The entire book
centers on their efforts to outsmart each other, and we know
going in that one of them, or maybe even both, will fail. Conflict is necessary in every book because that's what generates
concern for and interest in our characters. But we especially
need it in this story because without it, we don't have much of
a thriller.

Fair enough. We've got our conflict. But in order to lend
some depth to this story, maybe we want to expand Maud's
problems beyond her impending confrontation with her nemesis. Maybe Maud has lost the steely determination that once
served her so well as a CIA operative. Maybe her life is different enough that, like the sheriff in *High Noon*, she doesn't
want to have to face another showdown. So now we have an
opportunity to watch her wrestle with her fears and doubts,
even as she awaits the inevitable appearance of Feral Finch.
Maybe she is afraid for her cats or one of her friends or neigh-
bors and must carry the burden of their safety on her aging
shoulders, as well. Maybe she has just discovered she is going
blind, and her sight comes and goes at inappropriate moments,
leaving her particularly vulnerable to an attack. The more complex and overwhelming the threat to a protagonist, the better
the opportunity for the author to create a compelling conflict
and a dramatic resolution.

Of course, you can overdo this. Too many threats make the
story unbelievable. Too much conflict renders it unrealistic. As
with all things, you have to find a balance that works.

The fourth rule ties right into the first three: MOVEMENT

EQUALS GROWTH; GROWTH EQUALS CHANGE; WITHOUT CHANGE, NOTHING HAPPENS.

Uh-oh. I can read the confusion on your faces from here. The last part of this equation is self-explanatory. I think we all agree that changes in the lives of characters are necessary for the reader to feel that the journey traveled from beginning to end in a book has been worthwhile. But what about the rest of it? What the heck does all that mean?

Let's start with the word *movement* and see if the mystery won't come clear. When I use the word here, I am speaking of the sort of movement that takes place in the lives of characters during the course of a book. That movement can take many different forms. In some books, the movement is of a purely physical nature. The characters are on a quest that requires them to travel a great distance, or they are situated in a strange place that requires them to move around to understand what is happening. In other books, no one goes much of anywhere, and the movement is all emotional or even psychological. The characters are discovering truths about themselves or others that they hadn't recognized before. They are coming to terms with their lives through events and circumstances or through their interaction with other characters. Maybe they never even leave their houses, but they are moving about inside their own heads, nevertheless.

What matters is that in each case, whether the movement is physical or emotional or psychological, the result is that some form of growth takes place with the characters involved. Again, it might be physical—a coming of age that results in a transition from child to adult, a literal growing up. It might also be a coming of age that takes place emotionally or psycho- logically, one that involves maturity of thought, and takes place inside the person involved. Or it might be a kind of recognition of truths that becomes life-transforming.

But without that movement to trigger that growth and that growth to cause that change, we don't have a very compelling story. The reader wants to see something happen between pages one and four hundred, and as the rule points out, nothing happens if the characters don't change. I would suggest that this is the single biggest problem with series in all categories of fiction writing. From one book to the next, the characters don't ever change, don't ever grow, and don't ever surprise. They turn static, and when that happens you can be pretty sure the writer has lost interest in what he or she is doing.

So in *Cat Chaser*, even if we don't see this as more than a single book, Maud needs to evolve in some measurable way. She needs to do more than sit around fretting about the coming of Feral. Engaging in a successful confrontation that frees her from her worries isn't enough. She has to do more. She has to come to terms with who and what she is, what it means to her to have to fight that last battle, and how she is likely to go on with things once it is over. The reader wants some enlightenment on these issues, some sense of the humanity of the character, and if the author doesn't provide it, the story loses a great deal of its impact.

Part of the way in which we writers achieve all this is through the relationship we create between our protagonist and antagonist. Thus, our fifth rule: THE STRENGTH OF THE PROTAGONIST IS MEASURED BY THE THREAT OF THE ANTAGONIST.

The stronger the threat posed by the antagonist, the greater the demands placed on the protagonist, to put it another way. If we are to be compelled by what happens to our main character over the course of the story, we must see him or her challenged in an appropriately demonstrable way. We don't want to read some four hundred pages only to discover the obstacles faced were never really much of anything after all. This doesn't mean we have to see a protagonist placed in a life-and-death situation every time out in order not to be disappointed. It means that given the nature of the story, the conflict facing the protagonist must be real and challenging.

Don't forget that the antagonist in a story isn't always a person. It might be an animal or a monster. It might be an appliance or a vehicle; Stephen King has written more than a few of those. It might be the weather or a mountain or an inhospitable climate. It might be an impending cataclysmic event, like a nuclear explosive on the verge of detonation. It might be a disfiguring injury or a life-threatening disease. But in each instance, the size of the threat—its immediacy, perversity, potential consequences, and so on—will provide a way to measure the courage, resolve, and strength of character of our protagonist.

So Maud Manx must be made to rise to the nature of the threat posed by Feral Finch, by the fears and doubts his coming engenders, and by the limitations placed on her by age and disability. How successful I am at depicting all this will determine how engaged the reader becomes in the story, how compelled by the action, and how concerned for the story's outcome. Ultimately, it will determine whether or not the book works as a thriller.

Whew! All those other chapters were so short, and this one is only half done! At least it's the tougher half. It gets much easier from here. Nevertheless, let's take a break in case you want to turn out the lights and get some sleep, and we'll pick up on things in the next chapter. I'll go put out the cat.

*Readers will accept almost anything from
you if you don't make them feel they
have wasted their time and money.*

MAUD MANX,
PART TWO

WELL, HERE WE are again, back in our virtual classroom, ready for another look at those valuable rules of writing. I know I shouldn't say this, but even though I believe strongly in their value, some of them may not work for you. This is true about all writing rules and all books on writing, and you have to be able to pull out what will help *you* and discard what doesn't. Of course, I think my advice is pretty good, but oddly enough, other writers feel the same way about their advice. Such is life. You have to make up your own mind.

Anyway, back to Maud Manx, Feral Finch, and their adventures in the thriller *Cat Chaser*.

The single most violated rule of writing is the one I want

to talk about next, and you ignore me in this instance at your peril.

Rule six goes like this: SHOW, DON'T TELL.

I'll bet you've heard that one before. Almost everyone has. Certainly everyone who comes into one of my classes on writing fiction has. Three little words, and they seem to cause writers a world of trouble.

What those words are saying is that writers need to remember that the less we see of them during the course of their stories, the better. It is the characters and the plot of a book that are involving, not the writer. The writer needs to reveal the story through the words and actions of the characters, not through his or her narration of them. Everything that happens in a book should take place as if the writer wasn't present. We should be able to read a story through from beginning to end without any awareness at all of an author presence.

The problem arises when the writer violates the Show, Don't Tell rule. What happens is that the writer starts *telling* us about characters and events, rather in the way of the Chorus in the old Greek tragedies, instead of *showing* us through a depiction of the action. When this happens, the story stops dead in its tracks and starts to take on the look and feel of a lecture. Because the writer is now telling us what is happening instead of showing us, the reader becomes distanced and no longer feels a part of the story, is made more a viewer than a participant. The immediacy of the storytelling is stolen away. The spontaneity and life disappear.

To illustrate what I mean, let me give you two examples of the same scene. The first violates the Show, Don't Tell rule; the second doesn't. We'll use a scene out of *Cat Chaser* to illustrate the difference.

EXAMPLE 1: Maud was eighty-one years of age with piercing dark eyes and a stiff, squared-away stance that suggested aching joints. Gray hair hung in a single braid down her back, tied at the end with a ribbon. Deep age lines marked her strong, plain face. She was missing her right arm, the sleeve of her cotton dress pinned up against the breast and neatly folded at the elbow. For many years, she had worked in a bookstore, and before that, as a CIA operative. She loved cats and had two old toms at present named Kibbles and Bits. But while cats were welcome in her home, birds were not. She hated birds because as a child she had always been afraid of their beady, quick eyes and sharp little beaks.

Okay, that's pretty dreadful, I grant you. But I need to make the distinction between telling and showing as clear as possible, so I am going overboard just a bit.

EXAMPLE 2: Maud moved gingerly today, the result of another twenty-four hours added to her eighty-one years. Oddly enough, she felt the same as always, although her dark eyes might give her away to someone who looked closely enough. Ignoring her stiffness and the ache of her joints, she brushed lightly at her braided gray hair and smiled at the sunlight streaming through her cabin window. The smile gave her lined face a warm and reassuring cast, the sort that always suggested to those she encountered that she had a good heart. Kibbles, the better half of Bits, trotted up to her, and she picked up the old tom and held him in the cradle of her good left arm. She glanced down at the empty right sleeve of her dress, checking her appearance the way she had been taught to do during her years with the CIA. Government agents never forgot their training. Or maybe it was booksellers who never forgot, she couldn't remember. She laughed silently at herself, able to push back the years and the past. On a day like this, she could even feel kindly toward birds, and that was rare indeed.

I probably could do better if I wanted to spend more time on it, but you get the general idea. The second paragraph is more fluid and more fully developed. We learn about Maud through her actions—the picking up of Kibbles, her smile, her laugh, her reaction to what she sees, even the way she moves around the room. We learn about her through her thoughts. In the first example, we learn about her through a writer's bare-bones recitation of her attributes and limitations, and we are very much aware that the writer isn't showing us anything, he's telling us.

Which brings us to rule number seven: AVOID THE GROCERY-LIST APPROACH TO DESCRIBING CHARACTERS.

You know, remember to pick up the eggs, ham, bread, milk, Swiss cheese, and so on and so forth. If you take a look at our first example, the one that involves so much telling, you will notice that we learn about Maud through what amounts to a grocery list of characteristics. It reads like the author is checking off each item very much the way you do when shopping in a grocery store. How much more interesting and involving to work all this in through the narrative form employed in the second example, the one that involves showing us Maud through her movement and thinking. We still get everything on the list, but we don't have the feeling that everything we learn is being doled out in accordance with some mysterious agenda. We have more of a narrative flow and thus better storytelling.

I am not going to try to tell you that I have never violated either of these last two rules; I have. I expect all professional writers have at some point. But it helps to be aware of the probable consequences of doing so and to minimize the times you let one of these unfortunate lapses occur. To be good writers, we have to be wary of the bad habits that try to seduce us. We have to remember to look for them, to recognize them when they creep into our prose, and to banish them summarily. You can see for yourself the results of such diligence from the examples above.

Next up on our list of rules is one that is easy to apply and tough to enforce. Rule eight is this: CHARACTERS MUST ALWAYS BE IN A STORY FOR A REASON.

I like to think of my characters as actors on a stage, auditioning for a part. Some of them are quite good and very interesting, and I really feel they have something to contribute to the life of the stage. But what they offer isn't always right for the story at hand. Sometimes you just have to tell them that they gave a great reading, but that you don't have a part for them in this book and will call them back for the next. Meantime, it's back to central casting they must go.

You might remember that I mentioned this rule earlier in passing in the chapter on dream time. No matter how much I like a character—love a character, for that matter—I will not put him in a book if he doesn't serve a measurable purpose. By measurable purpose, I mean that characters must do something to advance the story. In a very demonstrable way, they must contribute directly to the movement of the plot. If they are just standing around looking good and sucking up air, they are out of there. If they are providing nothing more than decorative filler, no matter how charming they might be, they are history.

I am ruthless about this. Sometimes I will find a way to keep a character in a story by changing the plot so that the character can directly contribute. But sometimes a character just doesn't belong and has to step back and wait for the right book.

Why is this so crucial? Why not give a charming, memorable character a place in your story? Doesn't that add verisimilitude and color to the narrative? Yes, of course it does. The trouble is, it does a couple of other things, as well, and neither of them is good.

First, if the presence of the character doesn't advance the story, it necessarily stops it in its tracks. All of a sudden, you are going nowhere, your pacing disrupted, your focus shifted from the important characters and plot to this intruder. The reader's attention shifts, as well, and by letting that happen you are creating expectations you probably can't fulfill. If this character is so wonderful, when will he or she do something that matters to the outcome of the story? When will this character prove important to the way in which the story develops? The reader will look for answers to these questions, and if you don't provide them, you will necessarily disappoint their valid expectations.

Second, by populating your story with characters who don't contribute to its advancement, you risk diminishing the role of characters who do. If you draw attention away from the characters who matter, the ones who are in the story for a discernible reason, you may find readers losing track of whom the story is really about, or worse, wishing it were about the characters it isn't! It reminds me of the way a magician distracts the audience from what matters by doing something obvious. The difference, of course, is that in the case of the magician the distraction serves a valid purpose. In the end, the distraction is integral to the performance of the trick. That isn't true in the case of the writer, because the colorful character with which he has become enamored isn't going to be connected in the end to anything.

So what does this mean in practical terms? How would this rule apply in the case of the characters in *Cat Chaser*?

We don't have to ponder the importance of the roles of our protagonist and antagonist, which are pretty well determined going in. But we do have to consider our supporting cast. At present, there are three: little Johnny Gazette, the paperboy; Alfred Stamp, the postman; and Martha Handy, the woodswoman. There are also the cats, Kibbles and Bits, but I'll let you skate on animals if they at least provide comfort and occasional entertainment for the other characters.

There are a vast number of reasons for these characters to be in the book. They could be there to help illuminate the character of Maud. They could be there to provide a key role in helping her overcome Feral. They could be there as conversational partners for either, letting us shift from narrative to dialogue at crucial points. They could be there as cannon fodder. This is a thriller, after all. Someone is going to have to bite the dust fairly early on, and it would help if it were someone both Maud and the reader cared about.

For example, Martha Handy might be widely regarded as a nut case by the local populace, but prove to be invaluable to

Maud in helping her come to terms with her fears and doubts about her lapsed survival skills, offering fresh advice on woods lore or trap setting. Maybe little Johnny Gazette, in the course of his rounds, notices something that will help Maud discover what Feral is planning for her. Alfred Stamp might turn out to be cannon fodder, but in the course of giving up his life, does something that saves Maud's.

Once again, you get the point. No matter what you decide about the purpose of your characters in your book, the important thing to remember is that they need to have one.

An important corollary to this rule, one that bears at least a mention, is that the attributes you assign to your characters should serve a purpose, as well. I am not speaking of mundane characteristics such as hair and eye color or size and weight. I am talking about attributes that set your characters apart from everyone else. These shouldn't be assigned haphazardly and never just because you think it sounds neat. For example, if I take away Maud's arm, that loss had better have something to do with either character development or conflict resolution during the course of the book. If Martha Handy is a woodswoman familiar with homespun skills and remedies, that needs to bear in some way on her place in the book. Giving characters odd attributes that seem to signify something important about their presence in the story should fulfill readers' expectations in the same way that the presence of the characters themselves do.

Let's move on and take a quick look at rule nine: NAMES ARE IMPORTANT.

You would think this would be obvious, but I find more often than not that it isn't. Maybe part of the problem comes from not understanding what it is that names should do—

because they should definitely do more than act as convenient labels. This is true not only of names of characters, but of places and things, as well. Names should serve two very specific ends. They should feel right for the type of story being told, and they should suggest something about the person, place, or thing they are attached to.

I am acutely aware of this because of the type of fiction I write. In fantasy, where whole worlds are created from scratch, the writer has to give the reader a sense of both differentness and similarity. Readers have to be able to get a handle on what an imaginary world is like, which means they have to be able to recognize how it resembles our own and at the same time understand why it doesn't. In taste, touch, look, and feel, in language and societal structure, in geography and weather, in any way the writer looks at his own world, he will have to look at his imaginary one. I submit that it all begins with the names you use.

Even in contemporary fiction, I find that names are important. If a name doesn't feel right, it can bother a reader all the way through a book. The sound of a name, the way it looks on the written page, and the connections we make with it both consciously and subconsciously all play a part in how we feel about it. Sure, you can't know how readers will react to a name you choose, because you don't know their history with that name. But you can determine how the name works for you in relationship to your characters and your story. You can find a name that fits the use to which you have put it, at least from your own perspective. You can avoid the lazy writer's approach to slapping something on without giving it any real thought.

When I am asked where I get my names—something I am asked all the time—I say that I steal them. This is partly true. Maybe *appropriate* would be a better choice of words, but I tend to lean toward the dramatic. What I do is write down interesting names when I travel and put them on a big list. Some of these names come from street signs and storefronts. Some come from towns and villages. Some come from maps. Some come from ethnic sources. I even find one now and then when I do an autographing. Really, I get them from everywhere.

Because of what I write, I look for names that are a little out of the ordinary. I don't always end up using them just as I find them, however. I often morph or even combine them to make something different. When it is time to figure out the particulars of a new book, I take out my list and try to match up names with characters, creatures, talismans, places, and things I have conceived. Believe me, it is much easier to do this from an already completed list of possibilities than to try to think them up all at once. It doesn't always work smoothly, of course. Sometimes a name will elude me right up to end of the book. But it helps to have most of them in place when I begin.

So for *Cat Chaser*, I have given my characters names that are so obviously in keeping with rule nine that you can't mistake my intent. I wouldn't do this in a real book, unless it were a spoof, but I would want you to feel that names like "Maud Manx" and "Feral Finch" felt right for the characters in the story and told you something concrete about them. The same would be true, if less obviously so, about "Octogenarian," Montana. We all know what *octogenarian* means. But as applied to the town in question, I hope the name might suggest something more—perhaps a sleepy community the rest of the world doesn't much notice, where life is winding down, young people are leaving for fresher vistas, and old people are anticipating life unchanging. I would want it to sound a little odd for a town, yet somehow appropriate for this one—to sound, as well, just right for a place a former spook might choose to retire.

My tenth rule for good writing is the most simple and direct of all: DON'T BORE THE READER.

You can get away with breaking all of the other rules at least once in a while, but you can't get away with breaking this one. Readers will accept almost anything from you if you don't make them feel they have wasted their time and money. Remember, you can bore readers in a lot of different ways. It doesn't necessarily take a dearth of action; too much action can get you the same result. Everything in writing, like in life, requires balance. Cardboard characters, plotless story lines, leaden prose, and unfathomable endings will cost you readers, but so will impossibly complex characters, impenetrable storylines, purple prose, and endings so tidy they squeak. All are such clichés that it is hard to believe anyone writing isn't aware of their pitfalls, yet I see them crop up in new fiction time and time again. It is always a clear indication that the writer doesn't have enough respect for the reader. Readers may not be savvy enough to figure out what it is about a book that doesn't work, but they are plenty sharp enough to determine when they are being dissed. And nothing disses readers like boring them.

Preparation will help you avoid this. Organization in the ways I have discussed previously will go a long way toward keeping you focused on what it is that you are trying to do, and that in turn will help keep your storytelling interesting. So will liberal use of your dream time. Don't try to hasten or shorten the process; doing so will only cause you problems down the road. Writing isn't rocket science, but it isn't bricklaying either. You have to allow for gestation and rumination if you want the components of your story to develop fully. You have to think before you can write.

A good rule of thumb is this one: If you bore yourself with your writing, you will probably bore your readers, as well. When you feel boredom start to set in, step back and reconsider what you are doing.

There you have it—all ten rules. There are a lot more, but these are the ones that I think you need to remember. Pay attention to them, and you will have a better shot at doing some good writing.

*I was on record as saying repeatedly that
I would rather be tarred and feathered
than do another movie adaptation.*

THE PHANTOM MENACE

IT WAS LATE in November of 1997, just before Thanksgiving, when I retrieved a phone message from Linda Grey, then president of Ballantine Books, asking me to call her. I was on my way out the door with Judine to do some Christmas shopping at Southcenter Mall, so I decided to hold off returning the call until later. But when I got to the mall, I found myself standing about with time on my hands because Judine had wandered off to the lingerie department, so I decided to go ahead and call Linda back before she went home from work for the day.

I reached her right away. She told me that George Lucas wanted me to write the adaptation of the forthcoming *Star*

Wars movie, *Episode I: The Phantom Menace.* Would I be interested in doing this?

Two distinctly contradictory thoughts crossed my mind instantly.

First, I was on record as saying repeatedly that I would rather be tarred and feathered than do another movie adaptation. At every book signing, convention, conference, and public appearance of any kind, I had made this declaration. Vehemently. The *Hook* experience was still fresh in my mind eight years later, and I was not anxious to stick my foot in the bear trap a second time. No more movie adaptations for me, I had proclaimed. Not ever. No matter what.

Second, if I turned the offer down for no better reason than this, I could not imagine how I was going to explain it to my kids. The oldest was a huge *Star Wars* fan and the other three were rabid enough to be considered dangerous. Whatever explanation I offered, they were not going to understand.

So I asked Linda, who was not at Ballantine at the time of the *Hook* fiasco, if she was aware of the fact that I had sworn off movie adaptations. She said she was, but she insisted this was different. I said I understood. In truth, I did. For several reasons, this was enormously different. It was the most anticipated movie of the last twenty years. Everyone would go to see it. The exposure for a writer who did the adaptation would be huge. Hundreds of thousands of people read my books, but millions would go to see *Episode I.* If I took the project, I had a chance to reach them.

If I agree to do this, I said to Linda, I want to meet first with George Lucas. I want to reassure myself that working with him is not going to turn out to be another *Hook* nightmare.

Good, she said without missing a beat. He feels the same way about working with you.

I hung up the phone. What had I gotten myself into?

When I called Owen to find out—for with Lester's death several years earlier, Owen was now my editor—he advised me that Ballantine had bought the rights to do various books based on the next three *Star Wars* movies. Clearly, they wanted to launch the book for *Episode I* with an author who was not associated with writing *Star Wars* books. He did not suggest that I had lost my mind by agreeing to consider the project. To his credit, he did not even ask me how it felt to eat my own words. Probably, he knew. Probably, he had eaten a few of his own over the years.

I was scheduled to fly down to Skywalker Ranch and meet with George and the LucasBooks staff in early December. But first, a contract had to be worked out between Ballantine and my agent. I had learned a few things since *Hook*, and one of them was not to take anything for granted or on faith when dealing with movie people. Another was to have an agent, something I had not had in the past. Janklow & Nesbit now represented me, and Morton Janklow would hammer out the agreement with Linda.

The negotiation took place over Thanksgiving. I was back in Sterling with Judine so that we could be with my ailing father. We were staying at the house of friends who were elsewhere for the holiday. My father had gone back into the hospital, so Thanksgiving was celebrated without him. It was also celebrated in the midst of a flurry of phone calls from New York that suggested an agreement on the *Star Wars* project might not be reached after all. At one point, Mort called and asked me if I was prepared to walk away from the book. I took a big gulp and said I was.

What the heck, I had been saying it for eight years now anyway. I supposed I could say it one time more.

In the end, however, an agreement was reached, one that satisfied both parties. Afterwards, I broke down and told the kids what was happening. The huge fan kid was ready to pack her bags for Skywalker Ranch, and the others would have been happy to join her, but I reined them in. This wasn't settled yet. I still had to meet and talk with George Lucas and company. I still had to find out what sort of experience this was going to be.

I had one advantage this time that I did not have during the *Hook* debacle. I knew someone who worked with George. Lucy Wilson, whom I had met several times before, was the contact person with LucasBooks. She was the person with whom Ballantine and I would be dealing. I liked Lucy, and I thought we would get along fine. If she was indicative of the sort of people with whom I would be working, I could stop worrying.

Several days into December, I flew down to San Francisco, rented a car, and drove north to Marin County and Skywalker Ranch. I had directions to a hotel. Once there, further instructions would be faxed to me in my room. I was reminded of *Mission: Impossible* and wondered if I would get to see anything self-destruct.

Sure enough, at the hotel a message and directions to Skywalker Ranch awaited. I got back in the car and drove out. The ranch was situated in one of those incredibly beautiful valleys nestled in the hills off Highway 101. The entrance wasn't marked. If you didn't know what you were looking for, you would never find it.

Lucy met me and introduced me to Howard Roffman, the director of subsidiary rights for the company. I liked Howard right away. He was a former lawyer who had been with George since the beginning of the *Star Wars* program. I told him he should read *Magic Kingdom for Sale*. He told me I should read the script for *Episode I* and write down any questions I might have.

I was placed in a room where I read the script and made notations on a legal pad about things I did not understand or about which I wanted more information. (I already had a page of questions that essentially related to how I was to be treated.) I finished the script and my notes. I thought the script was terrific. You can't always tell, but from what I saw, I thought this was going to be a great movie.

Of course, I thought that about *Hook* initially, too, so I managed to curb my enthusiasm.

Next, I met with Sue Rostoni, who would be my editor at LucasBooks on the project, and several of her staff. They were friendly and relaxed. Already, I could see a big difference between the attitude of the people working on this project and the unfortunate functionary I was forced to deal with while writing *Hook*.

I had dinner with Lucy that night. She was quiet and reserved as always, but reassured me that everyone was happy I was writing the adaptation. I took her at her word. I was feeling pretty good about them, too.

The following day I attended a presentation given by Howard to a number of licensees who were seeking to secure various merchandising rights that would tie in with the movie. The format was a combination of oral and visual, with Howard giving a partial synopsis of the story and offering slides and brief rushes from the film. It was impressive, and the potential licensees sat glued to their chairs.

After they left, Howard sat down with me to answer what questions he could. I decided to be blunt. I told him my main concern was getting the sort of cooperation I did not get on *Hook*. I wanted to be reassured that when I asked about something, I would be given an answer. I wanted access to drawings and documents. If there was anything I was not supposed to know or have, I would like to hear about it now.

Howard told me not to worry, that this was going to be a different experience entirely. The Lucas people were going to open the vault; they were going to give me anything I wanted. This would include drawings of ships, characters, weapons, and scenes, and a CD that contained over a thousand stills from the movie. If I needed something more, they would see that I got it. I breathed a deep and heartfelt sigh of relief.

After lunch and a tour of Skywalker Ranch, I met with George Lucas. By now it was after three o'clock, and I was flying back to Seattle that night. Howard and Lucy took me up to George's office where George was waiting. He was sort of impish, stocky and bearded, dressed in jeans and a flannel shirt, and short like me, which took the edge off the size of his reputation and put me somewhat at ease. We sat down on couches around a coffee table and took out our cassette recorders, which we had all brought. It was a little weird, but that was okay.

The conversation began with me asking George if he was sure he had the right man for the job. After all, I didn't write science fiction. Neither did he, he advised. We agreed, after a brief discussion, that we both wrote adventure stories. I asked him if he was familiar with my work. He was. We talked about Judy-Lynn del Rey, who bought the book adaptation rights to the first three *Star Wars* movies back in the mid-seventies and believed in their potential when others did not. George had not forgotten. We talked a little about our past. I quickly became convinced that even though he was a California boy and I was from Illinois we had grown up with many of the same influences. He asked me where we should start our discussion. I asked a few questions in response, but he quickly suggested it might be easier if he just told me what he was looking for.

He said that he was interested in knowing if I could tell the story in the book more from Anakin's point of view. The original focus of the movie was going to be on Anakin, but it became too unwieldy to film it that way. Was it possible to change this in the book? I said I believed so. He told me he was looking for original material, and I practically fell off the couch. Was he asking me to add to his script? Yes, indeed he was. He began to diagram scenes he might like to see. Getting into the spirit of things, while still not quite believing what I was hearing, I countered with revisions of his ideas and suggestions for other scenes. We went back and forth for some time, trading possibilities. There was a fierce intelligence behind his arguments. He was passionate and committed to his work, and he reminded me of myself when he talked about it.

At one point, I found myself practically lunging at him to insist that an approach he was taking that relied on flashback was all wrong, couldn't possibly work, and shouldn't even be considered. I knew I had overstepped my bounds when both Howard and Lucy gave me a rather stunned look. But George accepted what I said without comment, and we moved on to other matters.

I asked if I could change his scenes around. He said I could, and furthermore I could keep scenes from the original script that he cut in editing. I asked if I could change his dialogue, knowing that what works on the screen, buttressed by visuals, sometimes just lies on the page and begs to be put out of its misery. He agreed again. I was both flabbergasted and elated by all of this. I asked certain questions about where the story was going. Mostly, he told me. He also told me what I could and couldn't use in the book. Some of what he told me was not going to be revealed to the public until *Episodes II* and *III.* I was expected to respect his confidences. I was just happy to have them for a change.

After a while, we went down to the editing room and watched film rushes. Principal shooting on the movie was mostly complete. What remained to be done was extensive editing involving the inclusion of all the special effects. What I was shown that afternoon was stunning. George made the console operator rerun the Podracer scene several times. I felt like a little kid with a new toy as I watched. George looked like that was how he felt, too.

Four hours passed, and finally I had to leave if I was to catch my plane. George said he was available anytime I wanted to talk. He said he would be in touch after a few final scenes were reshot.

I flew home on the plane, but I suspect I could have flown without it, given the way I felt.

George and the people at LucasBooks were as good as their word. I was given everything I wanted. I went back down to Skywalker Ranch one other time to discuss changes in the film and how they might affect the book. At one point, I called George to ask about the history of the Jedi and the Sith. He talked to me about it for almost an hour. Goodness.

I completed the book and turned it in by May 1 of the following year. It had been a dream project. Everything had gone as well as it possibly could. I was pleased with the book. So was everyone else. I had to make a few cosmetic changes, but that was all.

The book came out three weeks ahead of the movie and went straight to number one on the *New York Times* Hardcover Best-Seller List, where it stayed for five weeks. I was interviewed by every publication known to man. I could not have asked for anything more in the way of exposure. It was exhilarating and satisfying. George was kind enough to write a personal note thanking me for my work on the project.

There are a couple of things still left unsaid about this experience.

I firmly believe that George Lucas and I have written the same sort of story in *Star Wars* and *Shannara*. Both are epic generational sagas. Both deal with dysfunctional families and hidden secrets that will destroy some members of those families. Both use magic of a sort, mine of a traditional fairy kind, his of the Force. Both invoke magic that works in the same way, able to help or harm either the user or the target, with the result not always being predictable. Both are coming-of-age sagas involving quests and archetypal confrontations between good and evil. Only the trappings are different, his of science fiction, mine of fantasy. Both are classic adventure stories.

Could those who decided I was the right person to adapt *The Phantom Menace* into book form not have been aware of this?

In 1977, *Star Wars* and *The Sword of Shannara* were released within months of each other. Both books were shepherded through the publishing process at Ballantine Books by the sure hand of Judy-Lynn del Rey. She talked to me at the time about how important the *Star Wars* project would turn out to be. She told George Lucas the same thing about *The Sword of Shannara*. I could not bring myself to ask him if this had anything to do with bringing me into the *Star Wars* world twenty years later, but I cannot help but think that it did.

What the experience illustrates is that the people and events that will help our careers and prove important in our lives are not always recognizable at the time we first encounter them.

So I say to you in closing, May the Force be with you. It certainly was with me.

"No," I told him at once, closing the gate anew.

"The cats will eat the antelope and zebra.

You can't put them in the same pen." Hunter

looked at me. "But, Papa, they're nice," he said.

THE WORLD ACCORDING
TO HUNTER, PART ONE

IN SEPTEMBER of 2000, my grandson, Hunter, taught me an important lesson. He was not yet five at the time, my first and only grandchild. He liked making things up, acting out stories, and playing with figures, especially pirates and dinosaurs. In short, he liked to do exactly the same things I liked to do, which probably says more about me than it does about him. I am quite sure I was not acting my age when we played together, but I excused myself by declaring I was doing it only to entertain him.

Hunter was always playing at being someone or something other than who or what he was. Earlier that summer, while we were attending the Maui Writers Conference and walking along the beach to dinner, he announced that he wanted us to be pirates. He would be the captain; I would be the mate. This was pretty much the way the pecking order always shook down. *Say something,* he ordered. *Arrrgghhh,* I growled. He grinned. *Let's go in search of treasure, Matey! Arrrgghhh!* We swaggered down the walkway, trading pirate talk as we went. I get into this role-playing stuff pretty quickly, and before long I was firing cannon and boarding hapless treasure ships. Down the walkway we went, Judine and son Alex (who, at seventeen, wanted nothing to do with any of this) hanging back. People approaching moved way over to one side to let us pass, giving Judine sympathetic looks. I growled at them. *Arrrgghhh!* What did they know?

On the day Hunter taught me my lesson, he and I were playing pirates in his room with Playmobil figures. We each had a pirate ship on which to sail the bounding main. Hunter's was bigger and newer. Mine was smaller and had holes in the sails. Hunter got the good guys, the ones with sashes and tricornered hats; I got the bad guys, the ones with ragged clothing and peg legs. I was allowed two of the four treasure chests, but no real treasure. I was allowed only one parrot. I got two of the four cannons, but no cannon balls. I gritted my teeth and reminded myself that he was not yet five.

We played the usual pirate games. Hunter had books and books on pirates and he liked to watch pirate movies, so he pretty much knew what pirates do. They sailed in search of treasure, often stopping by desert islands to dig up chests of gold. They engaged in sea battles in which all casualties were immediately revived following the fight. Prisoners were transported now and then to Pirate Island, another Playmobil contraption, where they were chained in a cave, or they were set adrift on rafts and menaced by sharks, some of which came from Lego sets.

But in Hunter's world, pirates had a more colorful and diverse life than those we are familiar with from the history books. Hunter's pirates went on picnics, complete with tables and folding chairs, grills and cooking implements, and a family dog. They had a country home, which they visited regularly. At the country home, they had a dolphin pen and a spa. They also had a four-wheel-drive vehicle, which they took for rides, frequently encountering Godzilla. Sometimes they had sleepovers with medical personnel from the nearby hospital, who brought along an ambulance in case of emergencies.

Today the pirates were going to the zoo, which Hunter and I had constructed from building blocks. The zoo consisted of a series of pens containing the various species of animals. There was a pen for the big cats, one for the grass eaters, one for the primates, another for birds, and one more for the alligators and hippos. The pirates walked along the top of the blocks and looked down at the animals. They had a group of children along, which they had agreed to shepherd on a school outing. There was an entry gate and a ticket booth. The four-wheel-drive vehicle that transported them was left in the parking lot with the dog.

Hey, this is Hunter's scenario, not mine.

Halfway through the zoo visit, Hunter decided to open the gate between the big cats and the grass eaters and let them visit. I was quick to tell him he couldn't do that; the big cats would eat the grass eaters. I shut the gate firmly. He looked at me for a moment without comment, then went back to playing.

A little while later, he opened the gate again.

"No," I told him at once, closing it anew. "The cats will eat the antelope and zebra. You can't put them in the same pen."

Hunter looked at me. "But, Papa, they're nice," he said, referring to the big cats.

I then launched into a ridiculous attempt to explain animal behavior, which failed miserably. Hunter had no idea what I was talking about, nor should he have. Nevertheless, the gate stayed shut.

Until, only moments later, Hunter opened it yet again and began to move the big cats through. I was befuddled and irritated. "Hunter, you can't do that!" I exclaimed in frustration. "Haven't you been listening to me?"

Hunter, equally frustrated, put his hands on his hips, squared himself around, and shouted, "Papa! We're pretending!"

Oh.

Sorry, I forgot.

I thought about this later, chagrined that I needed my grandson to remind me what it is that we do when we play. How could I lose sight of such an obvious truth—I, who make a living at pretending and is supposed to know better? Without a second thought, I had disrupted the smooth flow of our playtime by shutting down possibilities simply because they don't exist in the real world. I was telling Hunter that he shouldn't do things if they weren't already accepted as feasible. I was closing off the faucet of his imagination so that he would conform to what everybody else believes.

I was reminded of something that I heard a few years back at a lecture on writers and books. The speakers were John Edgar Wideman and Terry McMillan. They talked about their approach to their writing and their view of publishing. I had forgotten most of it, but not one essential part of what Wideman said. He argued that our book culture is systematically devaluing the importance of imagination. He remembered when the *New York Times Book Review*, the premiere newspaper publication in the country, devoted approximately two-thirds of its space to fiction and one-third to nonfiction. That was now reversed, with increasingly less space being devoted to fiction all the time. It was representative of what was happening everywhere. There was a pervasive feeling among readers and reviewers that fiction was less important than nonfiction. We had arrived at a point where books bearing the words *Based on a true story* somehow had greater value than those that didn't. We were obsessed with "reality entertainment." If it wasn't true in the world at large, how could it have importance to us as readers?

On remembering, I was struck anew by the immensity of this pronouncement and its far-reaching implications. I know enough about the world to appreciate that the one constant in life is change. But change does not happen without imagination. Progress occurs not because we remain satisfied with what is, but because we hunger for what might be. We are always looking to take that next step. But the next step begins with looking beyond the possible to the impossible— because what seems impossible to us today becomes commonplace tomorrow. It is one of the primary lessons of the world, and it has its roots firmly embedded in the fertile loam of our recognition and celebration of the importance of the imagination.

Hunter doesn't know this. But I do. If I am to set a good example for him, then I must give him a chance to discover this truth on his own. I must encourage, not discourage, his use of imagination. I must remember that not only must I not close off the possibilities he chooses to explore—whether I believe them realistic or not—but I must encourage him to find a way to open the locked doors that bar his way.

But it is not only Hunter's imagination that needs care and nurturing. It is my own, as well. It would seem obvious that a writer of fantasy would not need to be reminded of this. But as the pirate incident so clearly demonstrated, I am as likely as the next person to fall under the sway of the world's overarching desire to remove the larger part of life's nagging doubts by embracing the norm. As much as the next person, I seek reassurance that some things are dependably constant. I want a modicum of stability in my life. I want a sense of security and control. Using the imagination can stir up trouble. Challenging the status quo of things sometimes evokes unnecessary concerns about what we've always accepted as true.

It is so much easier just to let things be. Big cats can't be put in the same pen as grass eaters. Everyone knows that. Everyone knows what will happen if you try.

Except children, of course. They think anything is possible.

I read so many books of fiction in which the author fails
to give any real time and effort to coming up with a
good beginning or ending that I grow discouraged.

BEGINNINGS
AND ENDINGS

I GAVE CONSIDERABLE thought to whether or not
to write this chapter, worrying that the subject matter was
too esoteric and my opinion too subjective. I finally decided
I should—had to, in fact. I read so many works of fiction
in which the author fails to give any real time and effort to
coming up with a good beginning or ending that I grow discouraged. It should be self-evident that both are exceedingly
important, that the function of each is so crucial to the success
of a book that a failure at either front or back is likely to sink
the whole project.

You think I exaggerate? Protest too much? Then here is my
defense. You decide if it's a good one.

We have lots of choices for how we spend our free time. Books are only one option and not necessarily the most exciting one. You can argue until you are blue in the face (and I have) that books are the best and most satisfying choice, but they are not the one most people think of first. Otherwise, more people would be reading than going to movies or attending sports events or playing video and computer games or watching television, and they aren't. Reading a book is the least visual form of entertainment (aside from listening to music), yet requires the most work from the participant. Think about it. If you watch television or go to a movie or attend a sporting event or a concert, all you have to do is sit there and let it happen. If you play a video or computer game, you have to exercise your thumb and a few fingers and in some extreme cases your brain, but you still have a screen to tell you what is happening. When you read a book, everything takes place in your mind. Not only do you have to imagine the landscape and the characters and the action, you have to remember it all for at least a couple of days or maybe weeks, depending on how fast you read.

We must also accept that we live in a time when speed is the central component of most forms of entertainment. Television takes place in ever-shortened segments broken up by rapid scene shifts and endless commercials. Movies and sporting events last no more than a couple of hours and rely heavily on visual movement for their allure. Video and computer games—well, you don't need me to tell you about speed there. That leaves books as the single form of entertainment that really doesn't happen quickly, even when the story is a fast-paced one, simply because it takes time to read and digest all those words and imagine all those pictures.

What all this means is that to a large extent other forms of entertainment drive the way readers approach books. Like it or not, or even realize it or not, they are influenced by all this fastness, this rapidity. I would submit that if a book doesn't hook most readers in the first couple of pages, they grow less and less likely as they proceed with the reading of it to want to continue. If they even get that far, I might add, because they might not get past the jacket copy when they first pick it up in the bookstore. It takes a lot to persuade a reader to take a chance on any particular book. (With my aging eyesight, I even like to check out the typeface.) In any case, once the choice is made, readers don't want to invest an undue amount of time finding out whether or not the story is going anywhere. They don't want their faith in the writer tested.

Writers can do so much to help themselves here, and they so often don't. The solution is simple. Get into the story. Jump in with both feet. Start with something compelling enough that the reader won't be able to put the book down right away. It doesn't have to be an action scene—a murder, a cataclysmic event, or a battle—to get the job done. It just needs to be something memorable enough to avoid the letdown of a too-slow, too-meandering start.

I began *The Sword of Shannara*, way back in 1977, with a long descriptive passage that set the scene and gave the reader a leisurely first look at one of the protagonists. Really, I meandered about for almost the first hundred pages. I got away with it then, but I wouldn't think of doing that in today's entertainment climate. A good opening needs to be immediately compelling. A good first sentence gives it an even better chance. Readers who are familiar with and have read my books will stick with me for at least a couple of chapters or maybe even all the way through, no matter what sort of opening I use. But readers who are new to my work are going to need a little more persuasion. A reading of the jacket copy will suggest if the subject matter is of interest, but if I get that far, I need a vivid, compelling opening to make sure that reader's commitment to the book doesn't waver.

The single biggest problem with openings is that writers have a tendency to want to begin at the beginning. They want to start where it all happens first so they don't leave anything out. But the truth is nothing starts at the beginning, at least not since the time of Adam and Eve. Everything starts in the middle of something else, and that's where it ends, as well. So you might as well jump in somewhere interesting as somewhere boring, and bring the pieces of the story and its characters together as you go along. Choosing the important components of your story ahead of time—and discarding the unimportant ones—will help you do that.

Endings suffer from a different kind of problem. Remember several chapters back when I was talking about outlining (don't cringe!)? Remember when I mentioned all those books by all those writers that were great for three hundred or even four hundred pages and then just tanked, all because the writer hadn't taken the time to outline the book in advance of writing it? Well, one conclusion we might draw is that bad endings suffer from poor beginnings. Another is that bad endings result from poor planning. The result is the same. What began as inspired writing some months back has suddenly lost its impetus. That memorable journey begun with such high expectations has meandered off into the wilderness. If the writer hasn't thought the story through before, now the pressure is really on. A good ending is desperately coveted, but not always immediately recognizable. Thus bad things start to happen. An ending that might not hold up so well under careful scrutiny suddenly looks like a million dollars. Or worse, the first ending that comes to mind seems good enough.

Sometimes, the problem is unsolvable. I discovered this the hard way with my late, lamented second effort, as chronicled in chapter six. I wrote that second book without thinking it through, and by the time I was four hundred pages in, it was too late to come up with a workable ending, because the rest of the book was junk. But even if I had written a good first four hundred pages, I would still need an ending that satisfied my readers and justified the time and effort they spent getting to it.

Think about it. The ending of a book provides readers with their final look at a writer's storytelling ability and writing prowess. It is the last impression they have of that writer. If the impression isn't a good one, it colors all the successes the writer has enjoyed up to that point. It mutes the reader's overall satisfaction with the story. It makes it that much easier, the next time around, to give that disappointing writer a pass.

It is hard enough to find a sufficient number of readers in the first place. Ask any writer working in the field of fiction today, and I'll bet they will tell you they could stand to have a few more readers. So why toss away a perfectly good opportunity to keep one you already have? Yet that is what happens all too often, with endings that don't live up to expectations.

It has been said that in the perfect scenario for a successful book, the ending should not be apparent at the beginning, but should be clearly inevitable and perfectly logical once you arrive at it. This symbiotic relationship between beginning and ending is what makes a book feel structured and well conceived. There should be a tightness to the storytelling that leaves the reader hungry for more because what was offered was so satisfying.

If I were given the chance to whisper like the proverbial muse in the ears of those writing or planning to write fiction, I would say one last thing. Don't settle for a beginning that doesn't feel strong and compelling or an ending that doesn't completely satisfy. Make your story arc the rainbow it deserves to be.

Publishers are supportive of the artistic side of writers,

as well, wanting their books to be critically well

received, but mostly they want them to sell lots

and lots of copies. Publishing is, after all, a business.

THE WORD AND
THE VOID

I N   T H E   W I N T E R   of 1993, an extraordinary opportunity came knocking at my door. My publisher, Del Rey
Books, offered me a lot of money to write a new fantasy series,
one not connected to either *Shannara* or *Magic Kingdom*. I
could write on any subject (so long as it was fantasy related) and
break the series up into separate, stand-alone books or keep
them as a trilogy. Because I was in the middle of fulfilling
obligations for books on another contract, I didn't have to write
these new books until I had finished the old, which would give
me several years to think about what I wanted to do.

Let me stop here and explain something to you about the way
publishers view writers. Publishers view writers as investments.

They spend time, money, and effort promoting their books, hoping in the end for a decent return. They are supportive of the artistic side of writers, as well, wanting their books to be critically well received, but mostly they want them to sell lots and lots of copies. Publishing is, after all, a business.

Mostly, it takes more than one book to "break a writer out" (a favorite publishing term for increasing sales dramatically) so that the books the publisher has been nurturing and supporting for all these years finally begin to pay off. When one book sells, usually the others start to do better, as well, and the publisher can anticipate the possibility of recouping its outlay and seeing a profit—so long as it can persuade the writer to remain in-house and not decide to take his newfound success elsewhere. When a writer produces a book that makes the jump from obscurity to midlist or midlist to best-seller, what the publisher wants the writer to do is to repeat the success. The writer can do this best, in the publisher's experience, by writing another book just like the last one.

You see where I am going with this.

When the writer decides to do something different, maybe only a little different, maybe altogether different, the publisher is usually not overjoyed. After all, it took time and money to break the writer out and build an audience for his or her work, and it was done, almost always, with a particular kind of book or series. Only a few contemporary fiction writers regularly write a different kind of book each time out, and even then they tend to stick with the same themes and types of characters. Yes, a handful of writers are so successful that no matter what they write, they are going to sell a lot of books. Tom Clancy, Stephen King, John Grisham, Danielle Steel, and Michael Crichton come to mind. They might not sell the same numbers as they would if they were writing what they usually write, but they will do well enough that the publisher can afford to indulge them. (Indeed, given the amount of money their books earn, a publisher had *better* indulge them.) But there aren't many of these, and all the rest of us made our names by writing a particular kind of book in a definable category of fiction.

So when one of us who isn't King, Steel, Grisham, et al., decides to move away from the type of fiction that the publisher has spent all this time and money promoting, a concerted effort is made by all those concerned with the business end to get the writer to reconsider. This is not to say they will flat out tell the writer not to do it. That would be like waving a red flag in front of a bull—especially where you are talking about a writer's art. You don't hear anyone trying to tell painters what to paint or composers what to compose, do you? It's no different with writers. Nevertheless, those with a vested interest in the writer will try to make clear the possible consequences of abandoning established ground for new country.

In all fairness, the publisher has a valid point. Attempts by established authors with established audiences to try a new kind of fiction usually don't succeed. What happens is that a sizable chunk of the audience drops away to wait for the next book because they read the writer for the kind of book that won them over in the first place, not this new stuff. Even front-rank authors have to accept that not writing the sort of book they are known for is likely to decrease their sales for at least one outing.

The reason for this digression on how publishers view authors is to demonstrate that Del Rey was showing a certain amount of confidence by agreeing to allow me to write anything

I wanted, even if the agreement stipulated it must be fantasy. Fantasy, after all, is a big tent. A lot of strange animals tend to wander inside.

I am not sure to this day what Del Rey expected me to come up with, but I do know that I was quite certain from day one what it was that I wanted to write. When the offer reached me I already had something very specific in mind and it wasn't like anything I had ever done before. I wanted to write a dark, contemporary fantasy, one set in our world that would address current social issues and incorporate a framework of magic that would fit seamlessly with what we know to be true about ourselves. I wanted to set the story in a fictional town in the Midwest that would be modeled after the town I grew up in. I wanted to talk about growing up—about how when we are children we believe in a sort of magic, the kind that lets us accept for a short time that anything is possible. I wanted the main characters to be a fourteen-year-old girl who could do magic and was struggling with her identity and a raft of family secrets, and a drifter who had been sent to find her because she might be the key to either triggering or aborting the Apocalypse.

It would be the kind of story that I knew would never work in either a *Shannara* or *Magic Kingdom* setting.

It would also be exactly the kind of story that would violate the rule I have just described about sticking to what your readers and the publisher expect of you.

I knew this going in. I also knew the probable consequences. I had experienced them once already when I did *Magic Kingdom for Sale* some ten years earlier. Even then, my audience overwhelmingly preferred *Shannara* books—epic fantasies in the Tolkien tradition. I had seduced my readers with those books, and they had come to expect, rightly, that this was the kind of book I would deliver each time out. When I wrote *Magic Kingdom for Sale*, they were accepting, but not altogether pleased. They liked the story well enough, but the most frequent comment I heard was, When are you going to write another *Shannara*? When, instead of doing that, I wrote two more *Magic Kingdom* books, it did not endear me. The consequences were these: fewer sales by as much as two-thirds, publisher and reader dissatisfaction in the change, and author disappointment that the books hadn't caught on.

Eventually, they did. They found an audience, and they gained acceptance from both the publisher and the readers. Now I am regularly asked, When are you going to write another *Magic Kingdom*? But it took some time and effort to get there.

And it did not involve the kind of money that this new series did, which I knew would color everything.

But here's the whole point of this chapter. Sometimes, when you are a professional writer, when you have successfully published and no longer have to worry about breaking down doors, you still have to make the occasional hard choice, and one of the hardest is choosing between writing what compels you and writing what makes money. The choice isn't always clear, and the one doesn't necessarily exclude the other, but in many cases you have a pretty good idea of which is which. I didn't understand this when I wrote *Magic Kingdom for Sale*, because I had never done anything but *Shannara* books and was still naïve enough to think my audience would follow me anywhere. But by the time I got to the book that would become *Running with the Demon*, I knew better.

Still, writing is an art, and artistic expression requires that the artist follow his heart. This was true to some extent with *Magic Kingdom for Sale*, but in the case of *Running with the Demon*, it was everything. I was passionate about this story, so much so that I told myself it didn't matter if it didn't sell the way everyone hoped it would. Not that I believed for a minute that this would happen, because I am as capable of self-delusion as the next guy. In fact, I thought this book would do even better than the *Shannara* books. I was so invested in it, so enamored of it, that I was convinced everyone else would be, too—even though I should have known better.

Well, you can guess the rest. I wrote what I believed then and now to be a really wonderful book—maybe the best book I have ever written. Hopes were high, fanfare was great, promotion was strong, and the book went right onto the *New York Times* Best-Seller List on the very first week of publication.

And then it promptly sank like a stone. Oh, it did pretty well, don't get me wrong. It just didn't do nearly as well as everyone, myself included, had hoped. It sold about as well as a *Magic Kingdom* book, but nowhere near as well as a *Shannara*. It got on all the best-seller lists, but it made only a cameo appearance. It was well placed in all bookselling venues, but only for about a month before everyone could see the handwriting on the wall.

As my contract provided, I wrote two more books in what would become *The Word and the Void* series, and neither of these books did any better than the first. But slowly an audience began to build, just as it had with *Magic Kingdom*. Readers quit wondering when I was going to do another *Shannara* book and started asking about the new series. Now I am as likely as not to hear from readers, When will you do another *Word and Void*?

Still, commercially, they disappointed.

So what is the lesson I took away from all this? It has to do with learning to live with unrealized expectations. Sometimes art and commerce collide in a way that diminishes one or the other. A writer has to realize and accept this truth. You can always write the book you choose, but you can't always make the readers love it the same way you do. I wish that weren't so, because I always think readers should love my books in equal measure. But they don't, and no writer can control that. No more so than a writer can control the sales a book generates. Readers will make the choices that please them, and that determines who sells and how much. When I hear someone gripe about how this or that writer sells so many books and they shouldn't because they really aren't very good writers, I want to say—Hey, the readers are the ones who decide! It's a democracy!

A writer can revel in unexpected successes, but must learn to live with crushed dreams, as well. If you are a professional, you accept both results with equanimity and move on. Another chance for either lies just down the road.

For me, maybe that chance will come in the form of another shot at *The Word and the Void.* I would like to do three more books in that series. I think the audience is out there waiting for them. I think the new books will be wonderful and will sell like hotcakes. The front money won't be the same, but that's a trade-off I'm willing to accept. I'll earn it back on sales.

On the other hand, those first three books will earn out their advances about the time I turn seventy-five.

Hmmm. Maybe I'll wait and talk to the publisher about it then.

Eyes shining, a huge grin on his face, he turned

to me as I huffed up to him, and said,

"Look, Papa! You can see the whole world!"

THE WORLD ACCORDING
TO HUNTER, PART TWO

I N   T H E   F A L L   of the same year that I was exposed to
Hunter's assessment of my view of the animal world, Judine and I decided to take him with us over the mountains to
Spokane where I was scheduled to make an appearance with
my latest tome at Auntie's Bookstore. This wasn't a journey I
particularly wanted to make, because I was in the process of
trying to finish the next book and I was behind schedule and
struggling. All distractions at this point were major annoy-
ances, and I felt I could ill afford them. Stress is us. But the
commitment had been made, so there was no help for it.

The event was scheduled for a Friday night at the end of
the third week of September, and I had also agreed to sign at

another store on the way back on Saturday afternoon. The drive would be five hours over and five hours back through some pretty extraordinary country, and Judine thought it would be fun to share the experience with our boy.

She always thinks these things, and I always think about the five hours I will spend cooped up with Jack and Annie. Jack and Annie are perfectly reasonable characters in the Mary Pope Osborne *Magic Tree House* series, a brother and sister who discover a tree house that can travel through time if its occupants simply wish to be somewhere else. Jack and Annie find a book that will allow them to do this and off they go, traveling back in time to visit dinosaurs, pirates, mummies, knights in armor, and others of the same ilk. Hunter loves the *Magic Tree House* books. Since he doesn't read, he listens to the audios. Since the audios play throughout the interior of the car, I must listen to them, as well.

Now, I know that Mary Pope Osborne, if she reads this, will understand what I am saying. It isn't that the audios aren't well done or interesting—for the first dozen times or so. But after, say, fifty times, I would do anything to make Jack and Annie take their adventures and fly right out of my life.

Hunter, however, cannot get enough of them. And in my house, Hunter rules.

So we packed up and headed out on a beautiful September morning, Jack and Annie at the ready. To my surprise, Hunter opted out of a *Magic Tree House* experience in favor of Godzilla. Besides listening to the Jack and Annie tapes and assuming the guise of pirates in various forms, playing Godzilla is Hunter's favorite pastime. It goes like this. We get in the car and start driving, and from the backseat Hunter tells me that Godzilla is chasing us. This is my cue to turn on the navigation system I purchased two years back to save my marriage, so that we can see Godzilla appear on the map as a flashing red dot. Hunter will then tell me that Godzilla is getting closer and I must drive faster. I will tell him I am going as fast as I can. Instead, I try various James Bond devices to throw Godzilla off. Oil spread across the road, for example. Nails. Rockets. Changing the color of the car. Turning invisible. Like that. But nothing ever works for very long, and Hunter always says, "He's still coming, Papa!"

Well, this is one way to pass the time on a car ride, and on this day we played the Godzilla game until I was ready to return to the *Tree House* tapes, which is saying something about the extent of my desperation. Eventually, however, Hunter fell asleep, which resulted in a modicum of peace and tranquillity as we crossed over the Cascades.

When we reached the Columbia River across from Vantage, we caught sight of a metal sculpture of a herd of wild horses set at the top of a plateau above a parking lot on the other side. Judine, who would drive miles out of the way to view the world's second-largest ball of twine, immediately suggested we stop and have a look. I pulled into the parking lot and we climbed out, looking up the bluff face to where the copper-colored sculpture was outlined against a clear blue sky. A few people had climbed up a switchback trail for a closer look and were in the process of coming back down. Hunter instantly charged toward them, yelling for us to follow him.

So we did. Remember, in our house, Hunter rules. We climbed this twisting, gravel-strewn, dusty trail that at times was so steep I had to resort to leaning forward on my hands for support. The day had grown hot and dry, and I was thirsty and sweating right off the bat. The climb was much longer than it looked, and much harder. I was wondering all too quickly why I was doing this. After all, I could see the sculpture already. I could see what it looked like quite clearly. I knew when I got up there that all I was going to see was more of the same, if a bit more ragged and rusted, from a slightly closer position.

But I soldiered on, because that is what you do when your grandson is calling to you to hurry up. We passed a boy and his mother coming down. They looked relieved to be descending. At least, she did. She gave me a tight, pitying smile as we passed on the trail. She knew what I was going through.

Ahead, Hunter was carrying on a conversation with some imaginary person, juking left and right like a running back, playing at something or other. I glanced back at Judine in disgust, and she gave me one of those dazzling smiles that made me want to marry her in the first place.

Near the top, with Hunter still a dozen yards ahead, a rattlesnake slithered across the trail. I yelled at Hunter, who stopped and watched as the snake disappeared beneath a cluster of rocks, and then charged ahead once more. Now I was genuinely worried, picturing an entire family of rattlesnakes lying in wait somewhere just ahead.

I put on a burst of speed—not easy at this point—to catch up with Hunter just as he reached the summit of the climb. He stood in front of the sculpture, which from close up looks huge, and stared not at the metal horses, but out across the Columbia River to the sweep of the land beyond.

Eyes shining, a huge grin on his face, he turned to me as I huffed up to him, and said, "Look, Papa! You can see the whole world!"

It was such a magical moment that I forgot all about the

snakes and the climb and saw only the look on his five-year-old face, shining with excitement and joy.

Later, I thought about that moment. It seemed to me there was an important lesson to be learned from it, but I couldn't decide at first what it was. Of course, I always think Hunter has important lessons to offer. Hunter is a kid, after all, and kids are always teaching adults something about life, even if they don't realize or even intend it. (Now that Robert Fulghum doesn't appear to be imparting any further wisdom on how everything he needed to know he learned in kindergarten, I'm thinking about writing a book on how everything I needed to know I learned from my grandson.)

In any case, after returning home to face anew the specter of my still unfinished tome, it occurred to me that writing a book was like climbing that hill to the wild horse sculpture. When you start out, you sort of know where you are going and what you will find at the end, but not exactly what the journey will entail. Certainly, there are long, dusty stretches in which you think you will never get to the top. Certainly, there are places along the way where you can trip and fall on your face if you are not paying attention. Rattlesnakes represent writer's block and various other forms of interruption that can throw you off your rhythm or bring you to a complete halt. But both tasks, if you persevere, are likely to culminate in euphoria when you finally arrive at your destination and are able to shout, "Look! I can see the whole world!"

I liked the analogy, but I didn't think that was what I was looking for. The real lesson lay somewhere else.

It came to me when I started to think about Hunter's reliance on and use of imagination when making that climb.

I watched him charge on ahead of me. He wasn't just

making a climb up a hill, trying to get from the bottom to the top so he could see that sculpture. No, indeed. Hunter was on an adventure. Whatever he does, wherever he goes, he is always on an adventure. I can hear it in those imaginary conversations and see it in the look on his face. He is living outside the moment. Like all kids, he is experimenting with life's possibilities, pretending at what might be happening beyond what really is. He is on a journey of discovery, and to the extent that he can manage it, he is making it up as he goes.

When I write a book, I do the same thing. I make it up as I go, a journey of discovery, an adventure in progress. The difference is that I have made the journey so many times before that I tend to be jaded about what I will find. I know all the zigs and zags I will encounter along the way. I know about the hot, dusty stretches and the rattlesnakes. I even know what I will find at the end, because as a professional writer I am supposed to be in control of my material so that I don't end up with a raggedy mess of unresolved plotlines.

What I tend to forget—what Hunter had reminded me of, even without realizing it—is that a large portion of what makes writing so wonderful comes from encountering the unexpected. To fall back on an old cliché, it isn't the destination that matters, it is the journey. It is what I discover along the way that I wasn't looking for. Sometimes a character will become more important than I envisioned. Sometimes a plot segment I hadn't even thought about will surface midway through. Sometimes the subtext of what seems an ordinary tale will reveal itself in such a way that I will be stunned and elated. The point is, even if I think I know the route, having traveled it so often before, there always exists the possibility of being surprised by something new. The joy of writing comes from that possibility, and the joy of writing is what keeps me making that same journey over and over without ever becoming bored by it.

A child doesn't need to remember such things. Or even to understand them. A jaded writer of fifty-odd years does. All adults do. A child's imagination, a willingness to look for the possibilities, is what makes life worthwhile.

At least, that was what Hunter taught me.

What strikes me as odd is that very few of those who choose to draw comparisons between Tolkien and myself mention the one that I think is the clearest.

On the Trail
of Tolkien

I T M A Y C O M E as a surprise to you to learn that I did not
set out to write fantasy. What I wanted to write, almost
from the moment I was old enough to make the attempt, were
adventure stories. But it took me a long time to find the right
form for doing so. Deciding what to write, it turns out, isn't
quite as easy as it seems.

I am often asked these days if I have ever considered
writing anything besides fantasy. A mystery, maybe. A legal
thriller. My questioner will point out that I was a lawyer once
upon a time—as if I needed reminding—so I must have some
stories to tell about the legal profession. My response? If I had
known how well John Grisham was going to do, maybe I

would have written legal thrillers instead of fantasy and be retired by now.

Of course, that isn't the way writing fiction works. A writer doesn't just sit down and write whatever type of book will sell the most copies in the current market. I know of only one writer who has written successfully to what he perceived to be the needs of the marketplace, and he did so only after years of experimenting with other forms. Most writers can write only one kind of story well enough to make a living at it. A few can write more than one. A still rarer few can write almost anything and expect it to sell, but you can count the number on two hands.

I have a theory about how writers work. There is a tendency to categorize writers of fiction as either literary or commercial. The implication is that either a writer chooses to write for the masses or the discerning few, for money or critical acclaim, for the here and now or the ages. There isn't always a clear delineation between the one and the other, and sometimes a book will achieve recognition both as commercial and literary fiction, but mostly not. Basically, this is how fiction writers are grouped.

But I don't believe writers choose their material based on how they think it is going to be received. I don't even believe that they make a conscious decision to write in a certain fashion. Rather, I think that writers just try to do the best they can with what skills they possess. I think they are imbued with a desire to write about certain subjects, and mostly that is what they do. It isn't a matter of sitting down and saying, "Okay, I think I'll write the next Stephen King thriller and get on all the best-seller lists and make millions." Writing requires passion and commitment in order to come alive. Writers write about what intrigues and compels them, what speaks to them in the same way it will speak to their readers once they find the right way to set it all down.

I cannot speak definitively for other writers on this matter, but I can certainly speak for myself. Perhaps you have heard the old saw that in order to be successful as a writer, you must first find your voice. Think about that for a moment. Does it mean that you have to find the right way of speaking through your stories? Or that you need to locate the narrative style within you? Or that you have to discover a form of storytelling that doesn't sound false? The answer to all three questions is yes. But mostly, finding your voice means that you have to discover what it is that you can write and write well. You have to discover that one type of fiction, that one area of storytelling that allows your passion and talent to provide the reader with a reason to believe that you both understand and love what you are writing about.

I came to my discovery of that elusive voice in the same way most writers do—through trial and error. I wrote many hundreds of thousands of words and the beginnings of many still unfinished stories to get to a point where I realized what it was that would work for me. I began my search by reading everything that interested me, because reading was my road map to the possible. Between the ages of twelve and twenty-two, my reading interests changed so rapidly that I could barely keep up with them. From Ray Bradbury to William Faulkner, from Jules Verne to Thomas Hardy, I read every writer whose books I could get my hands on. Then I tried to write like they did, experimenting with their styles and types of stories. Because that's what young writers in search of an identity do— they try on the clothing of successful writers to see if anything fits. Mostly, nothing does. But it is necessary to go through the process of trying everything on to find this out. This is what happened to me. I would read an author whose writing I loved. I would try to write like that author had written. I would lose interest. I would move on. Tales of science fiction, westerns, mysteries, family sagas, coming-of-age stories, and thrillers— each gave way to the next and none of them led anywhere.

All the while, I was searching for a format in which to set an adventure story on the order of the ones written by Alexandre Dumas, Robert Louis Stevenson, Joseph Conrad, and Arthur Conan Doyle. I wanted to write *Ivanhoe* or *The White Company* or *Treasure Island* or *The Three Musketeers*. Or all of them. But I didn't want to set my story in a historical context, and I kept thinking that using a different format—a mystery or a space opera, for instance—would reveal to me the setting I was looking for.

Then, in 1965, I read J. R. R. Tolkien's *The Lord of the Rings*, and I thought that maybe I had found what I was looking for. I would set my adventure story in an imaginary world, a vast, sprawling, mythical world like that of Tolkien, filled with magic that had replaced science and races that had evolved from Man. But I was not Tolkien and did not share his background in academia or his interest in cultural study. So I would eliminate the poetry and songs, the digressions on the ways and habits of types of characters, and the appendices of language and backstory that characterized and informed Tolkien's work. I would write the sort of straightforward adventure story that barreled ahead, picking up speed as it went, compelling a turning of pages until there were no more pages to be turned.

It was an ambitious goal, one that I did not immediately

undertake to achieve. Mired in college studies, I set it aside for later. It took another three years for me to pick up again, and then only after I became so bored with law school that I felt I had to do something to break the monotony and so went back into writing fiction as a diversion. Incorporating an unlikely mix of Tolkien and Faulkner to construct a framework and relying on characters and storylines similar to those of the European adventure story writers I so admired, I spent seven years developing the book that would eventually become *The Sword of Shannara.*

While writing it and even afterwards, I always thought of it as an adventure story. I understood that it was in the epic fantasy tradition, a direct descendant not only of *The Lord of the Rings*, but of the *Iliad* and the *Odyssey*, of the Greek, Roman, Norse, and Celtic myths, and of legends, fairy tales, and folklore since the dawn of Man. But at its heart, at the place where it meant something to me, where the passion and involvement found their touchstone, I always saw it as an adventure story.

My books are compared most often to Tolkien's, sometimes favorably, sometimes not, less so now than once, but frequently nevertheless. This is understandable. When *Sword* was published, Lester and Judy-Lynn chose to draw potential readers to it using words similar to these: "For all those who have been looking for something to read since *The Lord of the Rings*." Such language invites comparisons, good and bad. I have written nineteen books in three series along with two movie adaptations since I began my career with *Sword*, and the comparisons continue. I suspect they always will. It goes with the territory.

What strikes me as odd is that very few of those who

choose to draw comparisons between Tolkien and myself mention the one that I think is the clearest. Remember those pieces of clothing I mentioned earlier, the ones belonging to established authors that young authors in search of an identity seek to try on? Well, the piece of clothing I borrowed from J. R. R. Tolkien, the one I wear to this day and refuse to take off, is the one that defines my protagonists. Whether it is Shea and Flick Ohmsford from Shady Vale in *The Sword of Shannara* or Ben Holiday in *Magic Kingdom for Sale* or Nest Freemark in *Running with the Demon*, my protagonists are cut from the same bolt of cloth as Bilbo and Frodo Baggins. It was Tolkien's genius to reinvent the traditional epic fantasy by making the central character neither God nor hero, but a simple man in search of a way to do the right thing. It was the most compelling component of his writing, and I think it remains so. I was impressed enough by how it had changed the face of epic fantasy that I never gave a second thought to not using it as the cornerstone of my own writing. I had thought to see it used by other writers of fantasy after the success of *Sword*, but to this day very few have chosen to do so. Most still prefer to make their protagonists kings and wizards and men of power. I think that's too bad. Ordinary men placed in extraordinary circumstances are far more interesting.

In any case, it is in the nature of writing that writers follow in the footsteps of those who wrote before. Lester used to tell me that there are no new stories, only old stories told in a different way. Given the propensity of readers to want to read the same kinds of stories over and over, I expect that this is true. We are creatures of habit and seek the familiar and comfortable. Why should writers be any different? There is room for innovation and expansion, but that isn't the way writers usually start out. As with most things, we take the paths others have taken until we are comfortable enough with the journey to blaze a few trails of our own.

I wonder sometimes what younger writers think when they are compared to me. How do they feel about being told that their books are similar to those of Terry Brooks? I guess I hope that they feel much the same way I do when mine are compared to Tolkien's—that it's not a bad standard to try to live up to. I hope they remember that we share a common destination as fellow travelers on the writing trail—to write the best book we can, because no matter who we are compared to, at the end of the day how we feel about ourselves is what matters most.

If you do not hear music in your words,
you have put too much thought into your
writing and not enough heart.

FINAL THOUGHTS

THERE ARE A few last things that need to be said that I haven't found a place for elsewhere in this small book. They are directed to writers of fiction, but I hope they will be of interest to readers, as well. I have phrased them as admonitions because I feel strongly about each. Most are expressed in a sentence or two.

They comprise my beliefs about what it takes to write fiction.

Three character traits are essential—determination, instinct, and passion. Each has a place in a writer's life; each acts as a balance for the others. Determination teaches a writer to be patient; without it, commitment quickly fades. Instinct tells a writer which fork in the road to take; without it, as many wrong turns are taken as right. Passion imbues a writer with fearlessness; without it, no chances are ever taken. None of the three can be taught; all are a gift of genetics and early life experience.

There is poetry in fiction. If you cannot see it and feel it when you write, you need to step back and examine what you are doing wrong. If you have not figured out how to write a simple declarative sentence and make it sing with that poetry, you are not yet ready to write an entire book.

If you do not hear music in your words, you have put too much thought into your writing and not enough heart.

If you do not ever wonder what happened to your characters after you stopped writing about them, you did not care enough about them in the first place and do not deserve to know.

If you think that by having published you will become a happier person, you are mistaken. If you think that the finished book is of greater value than what you learned from the writing process, you are mistaken yet again. If you think the acquisition of money and fame is the most important reason for writing and publishing, you need an attitude adjustment.

If you do not proof your work sufficiently, both as to content and grammar, you must not count on anyone else doing the job for you. You have a better chance of winning the Pulitzer.

If you are ever completely satisfied with something you have written, you are setting your sights too low. But if you can't let go of your material even after you have done the best that you can with it, you are setting your sights too high.

If you do not love what you do, if you are not appropriately grateful for the chance to create something magical each time you sit down at the computer or with pencil and paper in hand, somewhere along the way your writing will betray you.

If you don't think there is magic in writing, you probably won't write anything magical.

If anything in your life is more important than writing—anything at all—you should walk away now while you still can. Forewarned is forearmed.

For those who cannot or will not walk away, you need only remember this.

Writing is life. Breathe deeply of it.

Photo by Judine Brooks

Terry Brooks is the *New York Times* bestselling author of more than thirty books. His novels *Running with the Demon* and *A Knight of the Word* were selected by the *Rocky Mountain News* as two of the best science fiction/ fantasy novels of the twentieth century. He lives with his wife, Judine, in the Pacific Northwest.

Printed in the United States
by Baker & Taylor Publisher Services